The History of the English Electric - GEC - Converteam Factory at Kidsgrove

1952 - 2016

From Valves & Magnetic Amplifiers to 25 Giga Watts of Wind Power...

The History of the English Electric - GEC - Converteam Factory at Kidsgrove

Nelson Industrial Estate
1952 – 2016

Mark Woods

Copyright © 2020 Mark Woods

All rights reserved.

Cover design by David Woods

All rights reserved. No part of this publication may be reproduced, distributed, or transmitted in any form or by any means, including photocopying, recording, or other electronic or mechanical methods, without the prior written permission of the publisher.

For permission requests, write to the publisher, addressed at the address below.

Published by Delta Power Systems Ltd

www.deltapowersystems.co.uk

570-572 Etruria Road

Newcastle, Staffordshire ST5 0SU

Printed by Book Empire

www.bookempire.co.uk

Unit 7, Lotherton Way, Garforth, Leeds, LS25 2JY

Printed in Great Britain

Although every precaution has been taken in the preparation of this book, the publisher and author assume no responsibility for errors or omissions. Neither is any liability assumed for damages resulting from the use of information contained herein.

Views in this book are the authors and do not represent views of the various companies mentioned.

SKiiP® is the registered trademark of Semikron GmbH

ISBN 9781913319243

Contents

Preface 1

Introduction 2

The Beginning 1952 4
    German Roots 8
    Activity at Kidsgrove in the 1950's 8
    German V2 Rockets and MagAmps 15
    Analogue Computers and LACE 18
    Expansion of the Site 21
    Geoff and Eric Reader – Life at English Electric in the 1950s 27

Expansion and Growth in the 1960s 29
    The Huts 29
    Westfields 30
    Northfields 31
    The Transistor Age 36

Computer History at Kidsgrove 40
    Early Computer Development 40
    The English Electric DEUCE computer 41
    The English Electric KDF9 Computer 44

The GEC Era 46
    Stability and Steady Growth -The 1970's 46
    DC Drives 49
    GEMDRIVE MICRO 51
    DC Drives Systems 52
    Southfields 56
    The Microprocessor Revolution 1980's & GEM80 61
    Major Investment and New Technology in the 1980's 62
    Training and Development 63
    Service Functions in the 70s - 80's 65
    The End of the Decade and the End of GEC at Kidsgrove 68

Recession, Decline and Downsizing 1990's 69

1999 The End of LV Manufacture at Kidsgrove	70
The Kidsgrove Works in 2000	71
The Years 2002 - 2004	71
CONVERTEAM & THE WIND POWER ERA	75
The Old Works in Decay 2005-2008	79
The Years 2008 – 2011	81
Semiconductor Supply Crisis and Further Strategy Change	84
2011 CONVERTEAM SOLD TO GENERAL ELECTRIC USA	85
2014/15 Demolition, Reconstruction and Investment	85
Kidsgrove Works – The End of an Era	87
The Demolition of the Southfields Factory and Office Block	88
Appendix 1 Timeline	90
Appendix 2 Site Plan	92
Appendix 3 – Company Logos/Letterheads	93
Appendix 4 – AC DRIVES DEVELOPMENT AT KIDSGROVE	94
Beginnings	94
Enter High Power – High Voltage Transistors	95
GEMDRIVE Spindle AC	97
The PULSAR (1984)	100
Pulse Width Modulation (PWM)	101
SL Drives and VF Drives – 1987	103
GEMDRIVE TB (1987) & SABRE (1990) DRIVES	103
The Move to Big AC Drives with the GD2000/GD4000 Ranges	104
Two Controllers	104
GD2000 & The Omega Controller	105
GD3000 & GD3000E	106
The GD4000 SIGMA Controller	106
GD2207/GD4160 and the Birth of the DELTA Module	109
Enter SKiiP®2	110
How the DELTA Module Operates	111
The First Liquid Cooled DELTA 1MW Wind Turbine	112
SKiiP®3	115

MV3000 – New Range of AC Drives for the new Millennium 115
Price and Size Reductions for Small AC Drives 117
The Start of the Large Scale Wind Turbine Business 118
Basic 2.3MW Turbine Converter Operation 121
Evolution of the 2.3MW Wind Turbine Converter 123
The 3.6MW Wind Turbine Converter 124
Conclusion 125
Appendix 5 - A Brief History of ICL Kidsgrove 126
  Beginnings 126
  Early Computers at ICL 128
  List of Computers 129
  PCB Manufacture 130
  Acquisitions, Take-overs and Mergers 131
  Demolition of the old ICL Works – Summer 2005 132
Glossary of Terms and Abbreviations 134

The site in the 1960s

Acknowledgements

I am grateful to all those who have provided material for this book. In particular I would like to thank John Pepper, Dick Wilson, Rob Fulcher, Geoff Mellor, Barrie T Jones (Canada), George Taylor, George Hart, Geoff and Eric Reader. Thanks also go to Rod Jones who contributed greatly to the Appendix on AC Drives development.

Above: View Looking down West Avenue showing the Main Works in the foreground and Northfields Office Block in the distance

Preface

In 2004, the company where I had worked for 26 years looked like it was about to close. Sales had dropped to a little over £10M and the workforce was down to some 150 people. (When I joined the sales were £86M with 1,500 employees). In order to record some of this rich industrial history I wrote a small booklet called the History of the Kidsgrove Works. The booklet was printed in house and given out to those workers who were interested. However, the company did not close in 2004 and remarkably by 2008 its sales had rocketed to £85M! This was nothing short of a miracle and the company survived a further 12 years with sales peaking at £120M in 2012. I carried on updating the booklet right up to the time the factory finally closed in 2016. The incredible story of how the company started and lasted for 63 years against the odds is told in this book.

When I decided to formally publish my in-house booklet, I had ambitions to also record the history of all the technical developments that the company had made. I started to list these and soon realised that each of these fields could be a book in its own right and so I decided upon a different approach. The first part of the book would cover the history of the buildings, site expansion and the main activities – pretty much as in the booklet. I then decided to pick only one area of technology to cover in detail which I put as Appendix 4. The area I chose was that of AC drives development. The reason for choosing this was simple. Firstly – it happened when I was there but more importantly, it led to the biggest sales volume of any product line in the firm's 63 year history. By its very nature, the story of drives development can get very technical and therefore it appears in the Appendix for those who are keen on technical details.

The first industrial building for electrical engineering on West Avenue was the 'main works' of The English Electric Co. with construction work starting in 1952. Over the next five decades the rest of the estate evolved making the site the biggest employer in the local area at one time. In its heyday in the 1980's the estate employed over 4,000 people and supported many more jobs in Staffordshire as suppliers and sub-contractors.

This book sets out to record the history and development of the site using archive material rescued during various moves and building closures so as to preserve it for the future.

Introduction

This book attempts to record and preserve the history of electrical engineering and production on the Nelson Industrial Estate at Kidsgrove, Staffordshire which began in 1952 when The English Electric Company at Stafford bought empty farm fields and had a great vision for the future.

In its remarkable 63-year history, the company which began it all underwent countless mergers, take overs, sell offs and name changes brought about either by government policy in the 1960s or by ill-fated capitalist commercial ventures in the 1980s and 1990s. The original buildings from the founding years are no more and modern housing known as Mitchell Gardens sits in place of the old main works, Northfields office building and huts. On the West side of the road, a huge modern warehouse complex occupies the site of the ICL factory. The achievements of the site should not be underestimated. Some of earliest and most advanced computers were built here such as DEUCE in the 1950s which helped lead to the creation of the giant ICL firm.

Automatic control systems were invented at Kidsgrove which went on to power the world's steel works and paper mills. Low Voltage Motor Control Centres were exported to every continent. In the 1980s, the GEM80 programmable controller dominated global markets with sales of some £16M annually and was found in nearly all industries from car plants, chocolate factories and even prisons in the USA. This decade also saw the introduction of digital electronics into the control of electric motors. At first this was an extension of the DC drives which had been developed in the 1950s from magnetic amplifiers but the breakthrough came with pioneering work on AC motor drives which took off in the early 1990s allowing for the first time, a fully regenerative, four quadrant converter in the megawatt range in the form of the GD4000. This work progressed in the next decade so that for a time, the Kidsgrove site became the world's biggest supplier of fully controlled wind turbine converters with an installed base of over 25 Gigawatts.

For my own story, I was only present for 38 years – or about 60% of the total site existence. I was not born in the first decade and joined the GEC part of the works when the site had been running for 24 years in 1978. I have been lucky enough to work in most departments including Personnel, Training, Test, Site Services and Sales and have lived through many of the changes documented here. I have also rescued as many old documents and photographs as I could so that the Kidsgrove story can be properly told. The desire in recent times was to throw out the old paperwork and erase the past and I have seen entire office blocks emptied and then demolished leaving only dust. Virtually all the photographs and documents in this book were saved from the skip and incinerator. My office became a sanctuary for rescued archive material and without it, we would not have much of a record that the 34 acre site ever existed as none of the buildings remain today.

Finally, the real story is about the people. Not just the great pioneers like George Nelson and John Sully but the ordinary engineers, assemblers, wiremen and women – up to 10,000 of them - who have produced electrical equipment that has powered the modern world.

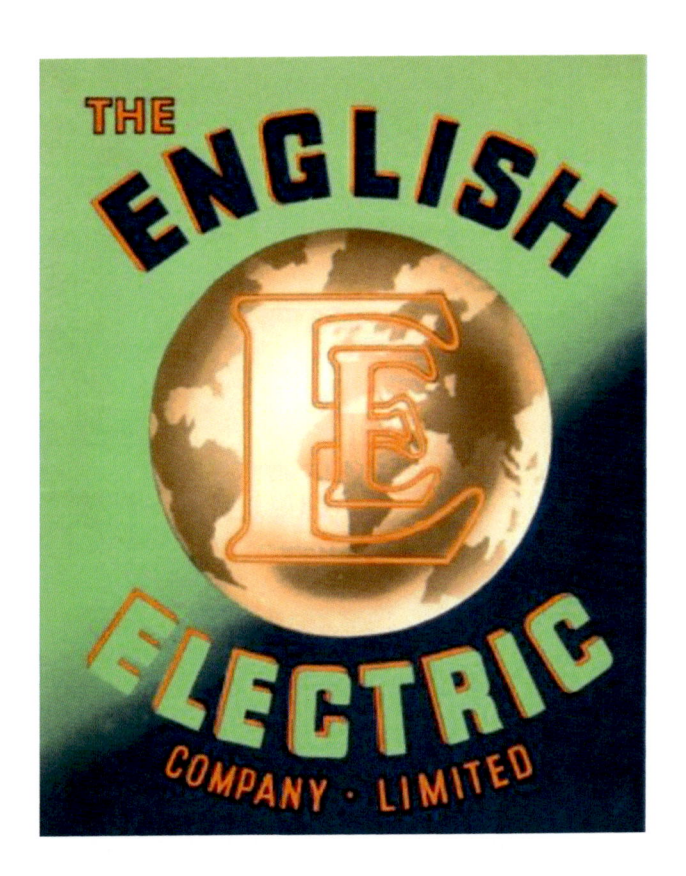

The Beginning 1952

At the start of the 1950's the Industrial Electronics Department of English Electric at Stafford (the former Siemens Dynamo Works) was expanding and looking for a new home. Empty land was available off Linley Road (A5011) in the district known as Butt Lane in Talke, Staffordshire. The nearest town to this site was Kidsgrove and henceforth the site was referred to as Kidsgrove Works although Kidsgrove town centre is about a mile away. Building work started in 1952 under the supervision of the architects 'Douglas J Oliver' of Mathews St. Rugby. The supervision from English Electric came from Mr TA Eccles. Chief of New Development and Process based in EEC, Stafford. The majority of the land was owned by Kidsgrove Urban District Council and was largely empty fields with some small farms, one of which was owned by a Mr Delves who eventually sold up. (Between 1890 - 1934 some of the land was used for coal mining as the Old Butt Lane Colliery). Some industry already existed on the site namely GH Heath of Macclesfield - a nylon mill (closed 1988) and an old aluminium works - Thomson Bros. of Birmingham.

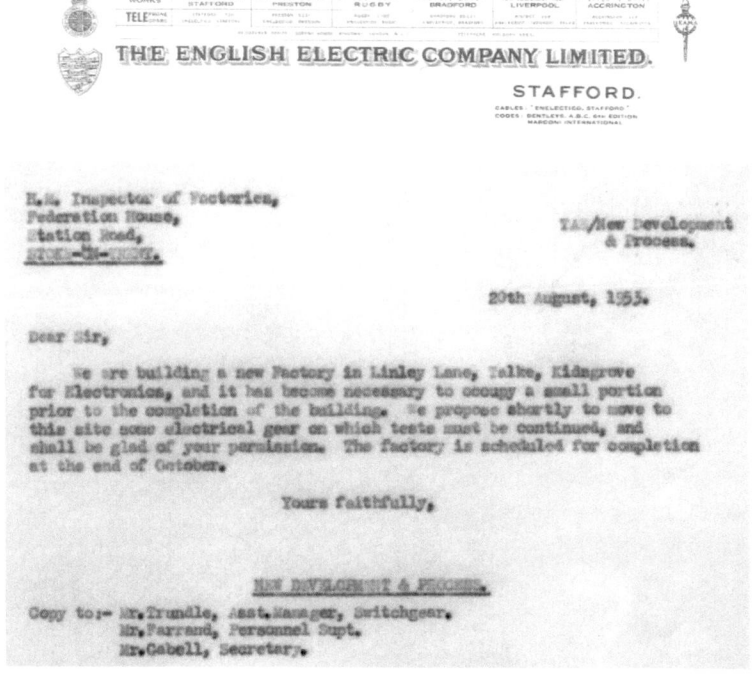

Above: Letter dated 20th August 1953 from English Electric to the local Factories Inspector "...we are building a new factory in Lindley Lane, Talke .... completion is scheduled for October"

WEST ELEVATION.

The new factory after completion. This view would have been taken from the fields that were eventually to become ICL.

The programme of work called for site huts to be erected by 25th August 1952 and excavations to start 8th September. During the same period a new road was built linking Linley Road to old Butt Lane. The road became West Avenue and was built by the council at a cost of £17,000.

The original land acquired was 14.8 acres and after tough negotiations a price of £8,000 was agreed! (This had been reduced from the original asking price of some £23,000!). Much of the construction of the main works had taken place before the land was officially purchased with the agreement of the council. The sale was finalised around February 1953.

The main works comprised the basement and what became known as bays one and two. The total cost of this work was £222,500. The work was not without its problems. In order to complete on time overtime to the tune of £10,000 had to be authorised. The steel used in the girders could not be supplied without written permission from the Admiralty in London due to the Iron and Steel Regulations introduced by the Ministry of Supply! Eventually all these difficulties were overcome and parts of the works started to come on line during late 1953.

English Electric at Kidsgrove was born.

FROM: M.H. FULLER, PEISER & CO.,
Memorial Hall Bldgs,
16, Farringdon St.,
LONDON, E.C.4.

Our Ref: RAM/PWS W.115A85.
Your Ref: SEC/GNG/SMP.

27th January, 1953.

Dear Sirs,

Land at Linley Road, Talke, Kidsgrove

We have had further discussions with the District Valuer and are now pleased to advise you that provisional agreement on the purchase price has been reached, subject to your approval.

The District Valuer's original "asking price" you will recall was £23,150 which he subsequently reduced to £15,000, and as we informed you this price in our opinion was excessive. At our recent interview with him we were able to reduce the price to £8,000 which we consider is reasonable. The District Valuer considers this amount is too low having regard to the sum of £17,800 spent in constructing the road, but in view of the Clerk to the Council's letter offering the land on lease for a term of 99 years at £20 per acre per annum or thereabouts, he is prepared to ignore the actual costs involved and assess the capital value on a market value basis. It will of course be appreciated that had you decided to take a Leasehold interest the Clerk to the Council would not have authority to assess the rent as Government money is involved and the District Valuer would be responsible for agreeing the rent. We do not think therefore the rent asked by the Kidsgrove U.D.C. is a true figure of comparison in considering the proposed purchase price of £8,000.

The Council suggest one or two minor alterations in the boundary and we enclose a tracing showing the extent of the land which they now propose to sell to your Company. The price also has regard to fencing liabilities as the District Valuer wished this to be made your Company's responsibility. We assumed that you would wish to fence the site in any event and so we raised no objection to this proposal. It is also understood that the land is subject to a small Tithe Rent of 19/6d. per annum.

We understand that the District Valuer is prepared to recommend the sale of this land, which comprises 14.8 acres or thereabouts, for the sum of £8,000 and will issue his Report to the Local Authority upon receiving confirmation that this amount meets with your approval. We shall be pleased to hear that you agree and to conclude negotiations on your behalf.

Yours faithfully,

(Sgd) M.H. FULLER, PEISER & CO.

The English Electric Co. Ltd.,
STAFFORD.

English Electric buys first plot land for the main works at £8,000 in 1953 although building work had already started in 1952 by agreement with the council

View from the high ground behind the factory looking down onto Bays 1 and 2 of the newly completed main works around 1953/4

FACTORY DEPARTMENT
MINISTRY OF LABOUR AND NATIONAL SERVICE

Telephone: STOKE-ON-TRENT 44503

Reference EW/GT
Your ref: TAE/New Development
Enclosures and Process.

In reply, please address as below:—
H.M. INSPECTOR OF FACTORIES,
32 CHURCH STREET,
STOKE-ON-TRENT,
STAFFS.

13th November, 1953.

The English Electric Company Limited,
Stafford.

Dear Sirs,

<u>Kidsgrove Factory</u>
<u>West Avenue, Linley Lane, Talke.</u>

Thank you for your letter of the 11th November advising me that you are starting up one section of the above premises on the 16th November and that you will progressively occupy the factory from then on.

I am arranging to visit the premises at an early date to advise on any points which may arise under the Factories Acts.

Yours faithfully,

H. M. District Inspector of Factories.

German Roots

Werner von Siemens had established Siemens & Halske in Berlin in 1847 and his brother - Wilhelm Siemens (1823-1883) ran the English operation eventually setting up the Siemens Brothers Dynamo Works at Stafford in 1903. However, the defeat of Germany after the First World War led to the company being taken over by The English Electric Co. in 1918. George Horatio NELSON became Managing Director of English Electric in 1930, aged 43. He had previously been the manager of the Metrovick Works in Sheffield.

At the time it was thought that English Electric would not survive as it had old machinery in most of its factories. During the 1930's the main products included steam turbines, generators, switchgear, transformers, electric and diesel locomotives, trams, ships and steel rolling mills.

As the Second World War approached the company moved into aircraft production and prospered.

By the end of the war George Nelson had made English Electric one of the largest and most successful engineering firms in the country. He was later knighted for his services and became Lord Nelson. The site on West Avenue was named NELSON INDUSTRIAL ESTATE after Lord Nelson.

Activity at Kidsgrove in the 1950's

Activity at Kidsgrove was quite diverse ranging from the design and manufacture of portable instruments to control gear and systems - primarily for the steel industry. The computer age had just begun and English Electric started to design and make digital and analogue computer systems called 'DEUCE' and 'LACE'. Two parallel divisions emerged - one concentrating on industrial control applications called the Control Gear Division and the other specialising in computers called the Data Processing Division.

To support these businesses the site had a range of shared services including a sheet metal shop, machine shop and coil winding section to make transformers and magamps (see later).

Above & Below: Bay 1 of the Main Factory taken in the first year of production 1953

It is very likely that these units are high powered RF Heaters which are discussed in the account given by Eric Reader later in the book. This design would have come from Stafford with RF Valves from EE in Chelmsford

Above : The Despatch Section, Main Bays, 1953. Note the wooden crates with Mesh tops looking like giant rabbit hutches. As they are marked "GLASS" these must have contained valve based equipment

```
                The Telephone Manager.
                  Stafford Street.
                  Hanley.
                    Stoke-on-Trent.                                    JJS/MKW

                                                              21st.May.1953.

                        For the attention of Mr.Hanford.

Dear Sir,
                Confirming our recent conversation about the Telephone
Services at our Kidsgrove Factory, we will require the initial
installation to be completed in October 1953. and the estimated
forward requirements will be as follows:-

October 1953. (Initial Installation).
3 Exchange Lines, 1 Private Wire, 10 Extensions.

October 1955.
4 Exchange Lines, 3 Private Wires, 25 Extentions.

October 1960.
5 Exchange Lines, 3 Private Wires, 50 Extensions.

                On the existing site we have facilities to increase
the size of this Factory 250% and should this be carried out
there is no doubt that we would require a Teleprinter Service, and
in addition as far as your Kidsgrove Exchange is concerned we
would have at least 10 persons whom we would recommend as
essential Subscribers.

                With reference to your request for a drawing of the
Factory, this will be available in a few days when it is hoped
we will be able to mark on the position of the P.X.Board and
the 10 Extensions.


                                        Yours Faithfully,

                                            J.J.Sowerby

                                    TECHNICAL MAINTENANCE ENGINEER.
                                          (J.J.Sowerby).
```

A Letter dated May 1953 to the GPO Requesting 3 Phone Lines supporting 10 Extensions. Note the Planning for a 250% Increase in the size of the Site. Advanced Planning was a Feature of English Electric

1953-55

On completion of Bays 1&2, work on an MoD radar project, codenamed "Postal", was transferred from temporary premises at a chapel in Thomas Street, Talke to Bay 2. The design and manufacture of a range of RF induction and dielectric heaters with ratings up to 5kW was transferred from Stafford to Bay 1. Several laboratories and offices were set up in each bay dealing with development and design of electronic instrumentation equipment, peripherals for DEUCE and magnetic amplifiers ("magamps").

1954-58

With the increasing need for manufacturing space, part of the hill to the east of Bays 1&2 was cut away, exposing some old mine workings and enabling Bays 4 & 5 to be built, with a gap between the two sets of bays.

Sometime later Bay 3 was fitted into the gap, not without some difficulty, as the two sets of bays were not exactly parallel to each other!

Bay 3 was built to accommodate a test facility for DEUCE mainframes and special ventilation ducting was needed to deal with the several kW of heat that each generated. About five mainframes could be accommodated at a time.

During this period, what was known as "Valves & Seals" was transferred from Rectifier Division, Stafford to Bay 1 and ultimately to the basement. This was a production unit only, with engineering responsibility remaining at Stafford. The "Valves" (pictured overleaf) were small simple anode mercury arc rectifiers, the majority being ignitrons, whose most important use was for spot welding equipment. Much attention had to be paid to the perfection of the special "Seals" between the glass envelope and the external electrical connections.

Advert in the local newspaper for 50 trainee wiremen. Note that only *young men* need apply!

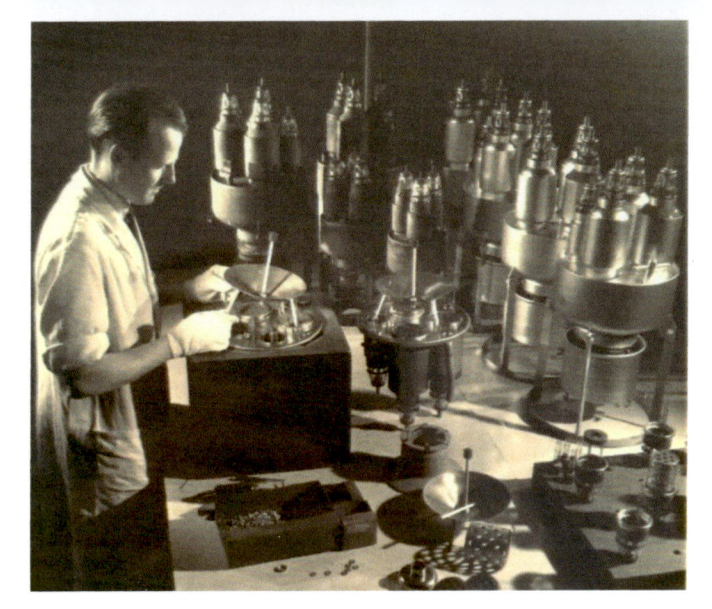

Valve Equipment at Kidsgrove 1950s

Building Work adjacent to the Main Bays 1 & 2. This is prior to the construction of Bay 3 and the Canteen Block

Memorandum from SWITCHGEAR DEVELOPMENT to CHIEF ENGINEER.

To Mr. ECCLES.

2nd November, 1953

Subject G.P.O. TELEPHONES FOR KIDSGROVE FACTORY.

Our Ref. SWGR.DEV.LP12/11/LW.　　　　Your Ref.

　　　　Enclosed please find one print of drawing No. SPK/085 issue A.

　　　　This print shows the positions of the G.P.O. telephone requirements on the ground floor up to the brick wall. The following additional telephones will be required to those shown on the drawing :-
　　　　　　Fireman.
　　　　　　Medical Room.
　　　　　　Gate House.
　　　　　　Modulator Lab. Chief.
　　　　　　Motor Control Lab. Chief with extension to R.F.
　　　　　　Heater Lab. Chief.
　　　　　　Superintendent and Development Engineer.

　　　　This gives a total of 17 telephones and 5 extra instruments.

　　　　The revised layout of the Laboratories and the position of the Superintendent and Development Engineer's office will be forwarded as soon as possible.

　　　　　　　　　　　　　　　　　　CHIEF METHODS ENGINEER,
　　　　　　　　　　　　　　　　　　SWITCHGEAR WORKS.

Another document regarding GPO telephones from the first year. This memo tells us something of the important people in the factory and their roles. Mentioned are the Motor Control Lab Chief, the R.F. Heater Lab Chief and the Modulator Lab Chief. This letter supports the view that the main activity in the early years were high power RF valves for heating and possibly Radar together with the more traditional motor control business.

German V2 Rockets and MagAmps

During the war, the Germans had launched hundreds of deadly V2 rockets on England. Part of the guidance and control system in V2s used the pioneering technology of 'magnetic amplifiers' for servo control of the stabilising fins. This technology was adapted and developed in the 1950's for use in industrial control. Magnetic amplifiers were the workhorses for power control of a variety of system applications, predominantly in steel rolling mills and other "continuous" processes. They usually controlled the fields of DC machines in Ward Leonard and similar systems. To achieve faster response and smaller size they were usually designed to operate from 400Hz supplies in ratings up to 2kW, being accommodated in withdrawable chassis fitted into control cubicles. These occupied much of the manufacturing space in the earlier years. The main 'magamp' toroidally wound components used for control systems were designed as epoxy resin encapsulated units of some complexity and considerable space was required for their manufacture. The actual coilwinding for these and for transformers was done in different locations over the years, at one time in the basement of Bays 1&2, with special facilities for resin encapsulation in one of the newer bays. Hundreds of magamps of this type were manufactured during this period. A considerable number of 'magamps' designed for 50Hz supplies in ratings 0.5-50kW were used for voltage control of DC motor armatures in 'stand-alone' drives. As these were of a simpler design, usually with only one or two control windings, it was usually not necessary to consider "potting" them. One of the key design engineers on Magamps was Mr John Pepper, who was Chief Engineer at Kidsgrove for many years and who has contributed to this, and other sections of the book.

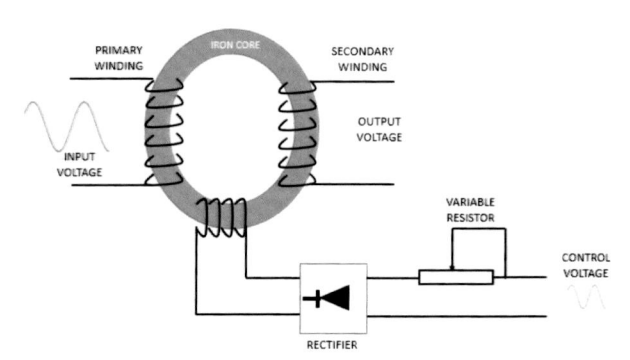

Above: Simplified Operation of the Mag Amp. A small control voltage is rectified and provides DC to a control winding on a special transformer. By varying the control voltage, the larger output voltage can be controlled

The Magnetic Amplifier formed the heart of control systems in the 1950s. Shown here is the assembly line for the Mag Amps and the toroidal transformer can be seen together with the big metal oxide rectifier being wired by Jim Mountford

Magnetic Amplifier Cubicle made up of Multiple Mag Amp Chassis Units – this functionality would now be achieved with a single PCB

1957

Investigation into the use of thyristors for power control commenced and it was soon apparent that thyristor amplifiers (converters) would signify the demise of magnetic amplifiers, at a rate depending on the development and availability of higher voltage and current capability of the thyristors themselves. Some of the control advantages would be lost and control system technology would need to be modified. This would be facilitated by the introduction of transistor operational amplifiers such as CA3/CA4, as envisaged at that time.

Analogue Computers and LACE

During the war, secret development work had taken place in the English Electric Guided Missiles Division at Luton on analogue computer designs. These machines were based on thermionic valve technology and were aimed at military applications. The machine to come out of this development was code-named LACE which stands for Luton Analogue Computing Engine. Production of the LACE was transferred to Kidsgrove in 1954 but the range was short lived due to the dominance of digital computers which are covered in detail later. The Luton factory was closed and was relocated to Stevenage - later to become an ICL factory.

Quite Possibly an Original LACE Mk 1 Computer. This was described as an English Electric Analogue Computer in use at the Nelson Labs at Stafford

The LACE MkII Analogue computer during test at Kidsgrove around 1958

LACE MkII with staff who are thought to be assembler June Hill and Engineer Ben Revell

Expansion of the Site

Major building work continued throughout the 1950s and did not finish until the end of the 1980's. (The last building to be built by GEC was N Block in 1988).

More land was acquired in 1954 including the area on the opposite side of West Avenue which became the computer factory.

A small section of high wooded ground near what was to become the sports pavilion was also bought. This land was purchased in anticipation that the firm would move into radar equipment and would use the land for the siting of aerials. In 1955 work commenced on the new Bay 3 to accommodate the expanding company. In June of 1958 an order was placed with Taylor Woodrow for construction of the new canteen block. The cost was £48,000.

VIEW OF MAIN OFFICE ENTRANCE FROM NORTH END.

Main Works 1953

Foundations Being Prepared for the Canteen Block 1957. Note the English Electric Van. Vans like these were used as a shuttle from Stafford to Kidsgrove

These pictures are from late 1957 to March 1958 showing the building of the new canteen block

J.R.SULLY. MANAGER. KIDSGROVE.

J.O.TRUNDLE. 15th April, 60.

M.1/JRS/EJ.

Mr. Nelson confirmed this morning that we should go ahead with the purchase of the 8 acres of land at Kidsgrove adjacent to the existing site.

We also discussed the land on the opposite side of the road (I believe this is about 6 acres) and he clearly indicated that we ought to acquire this also, primarily to ensure that in the future we never reach the situation where we would have to take a product away from Kidsgrove due to a lack of room. Mr. Nelson instructed that we should again consider carefully the building problems associated with this land on the opposite side of the road and, in particular, consider the building of the Computer Centre (as distinct from a Works Office Block) on this land.

He instructed that we should take immediate steps in any case to prevent this land being sold elsewhere whilst we are carrying out this exercise.

In brief, my impression is that it is highly probable now that we shall purchase not only the 8 acres adjacent to the factory but the other plot also.

For record purposes, the land prices we had in mind during the discussion were £1000 an acre for the 8 acre site adjacent to the factory, and £2000 an acre for the other site on the opposite side of the road.

J.R.Sully

GENERAL MANAGER. STAFFORD AND KIDSGROVE.

c.c. Mr.T.A.Eccles.
     Mr.L.G.Larke.

This memo from 1960 is significant in that Lord Nelson prepares for expansion of the site by the purchase of more land (to become Southfields and Westfields/ICL) to ensure "we would never have to take a product away from Kidsgrove due to lack of room"

MANAGEMENT OF ENGLISH ELECTRIC

Kidsgrove

1950s

Mr John.R.Sully	General Manager, Stafford and Kidsgrove (above) who founded the site
Mr J.O. Trundle	Works Manager
Mr M.A.Palmer	Works Manager
Mr W.E. Scott	Manager DP & CSD Kidsgrove

Above - coilwinding section, main works in late 1950's. Coils were used in numerous applications including single and three phase transformers and magnetic amplifier use

DRAWING OFFICE.

Above: All drawings were of course done by hand up until CAD became viable in the 1980s. This picture shows the set up of the Drawing Office at English Electric, Kidsgrove

Geoff and Eric Reader - Life at English Electric in the 1950s

The following interesting and detailed account of early English Electric is provided by Geoff Reader and his father Eric Reader who was Chief Draughtsman for many years.

"English Electric was formed in 1918 by the merger of Siemens Dynamo, Whylans & Robinson Rugby, Dick Kerr Preston Phoenix Dyanmo Bradford. In 1950 English Electric Industrial Controls (EEIC) in Stafford made the decision to move to Kidsgrove. John Sully was Group CEO at the time. The newly formed Industrial Controls Division of EEIC began in Foregate St Stafford in 1950 / 51. The first invasion of EE to Kidsgrove was not to the West Ave works but a disused St Thomas's Chapel on Coal Pit Hill in 1953. The building housed the sales, engineering/design while the production was provided by the main works switch gear division. Although The Division was titled "Industrial Controls" one of the first contracts obtained was the control of gun turrets for Royal Navy war ships - followed by a Photographic Paper Mill Control System for Kodak Ltd. 1953/4 saw the completion of the West Ave Site which grew rapidly. It was started by 80 -100 people coming back coach each day from Stafford plus a small number from Marconi Chelmsford. Mr Todd, for example, one of the earlier Chief Engineers came from Chelmsford. As time went by there was an influx of people from English Electric Bradford and to the Drawing Office staff from Brook Hurst Ltd, Chester.

The Division rapidly went from strength to strength, the early atmosphere was a great example of a company looking after both the hearts and minds of its workers and their families. This spirit persisted throughout the EE era. As GEC took hold much of the family orientated activities diminished. By 1967 there were 7,000 employees and 300 apprentices!

An extremely active Apprentice's Association was formed. This included 21 members on the General Committee. They ran a Rifle Club, Cricket Club, Football Club, Electronics Club and outdoor activities often in association with Staffordshire Education Committee Association of Youth Clubs. In the late 1960's Geoff Reader & Karl Hendrick edited the Apprentice Magazine "Contact". At that time they were "allowed" an afternoon away from normal work a week to interview people for article in the magazine!

In the late 60's they won a National Youth Associations Magazine Competition in London. The award was presented by The Duke of Gloucester. English Electric also has a strong Social & Athletic Club and an active Engineering Society. Sports Days Games and Children's' Parties soon became the order of the day.

Early contracts included systems for atomic power plants at Hinkley Point, Wylfa and Sizewall. Steel works at Colvilles in Scotland, our local Shelton Bar and the Steel Company of Wales were customers. Shelton Bar used its English Electric Controls during its steel rolling life from 1964 to April 2000. (In 1964 Shelton was the world's first steel plant using 100% continuously cast production).

Alongside industrial projects were two military contracts including "Postal 2" for Radar and the "Blue streak" guided missile. A more commercial venture was an RF Heater (fore runner of the Microwave) used for baking bread, gluing tennis rackets and shrink fitting fly wheels for the Ford Motor Co. One infamous project was the manufacture of condoms - these were tested in various ways – gas filled and released in the Factory at Christmas was one such test! During this time there were just the two long bays with the canteen in the basement. The "temporary" huts first arrived in the early 60's. English Electric Computers started by Anglicising some US RCA designs on the main site before being the first company sited across the road. The Joe Lyons tea house company came in with Leo (EE Leo) soon followed by Marconi. 1969 saw the Merger of EE and GEC."

Above : Senior Management team at GEC Industrial Controls c. mid 1970's. This appears to be a 35 year long service award group. Eric Reader seated 4th on Front Row

Expansion and Growth in the 1960s

The Huts

The start of the 1960's found English Electric becoming short of space and buildings. The workforce had increased from a few hundred in 1954 to 2,000 in September 1961.

During 1958-59 a number of temporary wooden huts had been installed at the back of Bay 5 (These were technically called Pratten Buildings but would always be referred to as the 'huts'). Planning permission for the huts was given and was due to expire in December 1961. In practice these temporary huts continued to be used for the next 30 years! The first huts to be built were called A,B,C and D blocks. They housed a total of 224 people.

Occupants of the 'Huts' in the 1960s

	No. Offices	Sq.ft	Staff
A Block			
Computer Service Visitors	2	800	-
Computer Engineers	9	3550	64
Control Gear Engineers	4	850	17
Conference Rooms	2	261	-
Works Accounts	5	1600	26
B Block			
Computer Bureau and Programmers	14	2752	33
Technical Writers	1	315	5
Control Information and Library	3	890	6
Conference rooms	4	573	-
Service Projects Section	2	516	15
C Block			
Typing Pool	2	651	14
Control Gear	4	2100	35
Data Processing	2	700	19
D Block - Lecture Room	2	1560	-

Westfields

In May 1961 the Chairman gave the go ahead for the construction of new buildings on the west side of the road - "Westfields". These new buildings, comprising of workshops and an office block, were to house the growing computer business which eventually became ICL. Some six acres of land had been purchased at a cost of £2,000/acre. Building started in July 1961 and was scheduled for completion by the summer/autumn of 1962. The factory part was modelled on the St.Albans works of Marconi Instruments Ltd which had been built by the firm Octavius Atkinson. The budget costs were £311,000 for the factory and £94,000 for the office block.

From 1963 a new company was formed called English Electric Leo Computers Ltd. In 1964 the computer interests of Marconi were acquired to form English Electric-Leo-Marconi Computers Ltd - quite a mouthful.

This new company existed along side the traditional Control Gear Division of English Electric in the Kidsgrove works - now on both sides of the road.

Westfields Office Block – Later to become part of ICL

Northfields

Both companies prospered to such an extent that more land and buildings were required. In 1965 employee numbers had risen to 2,700. In May 1966 a specification was drawn up for the construction of a four-storey office block to be located at the northern end of the site. This was to become Northfields. The contract - worth £213,186 - was awarded to Taylor Woodrow and the Chief Architect was Mr RG Pickering. Work commenced in July 1966 and was scheduled for completion in April 1967.

Above: Northfields Office Block circa. 1970 showing glass encased stairwell which was later bricked up

Next Page: Part of the Original Contract for Northfields Office Block

DS 17

PRIVATE EDITION (WITH QUANTITIES)

Articles of Agreement

made the __eighth__ day of __September__ 19 66

BETWEEN __THE ENGLISH ELECTRIC CO. LTD.,__

of (or whose registered office is situate at) __ENGLISH ELECTRIC HOUSE,__
__STRAND, LONDON.__

(hereinafter called 'the Employer') of the one part and

__TAYLOR WOODROW CONSTRUCTION (MIDLAND) LIMITED.,__

of (or whose registered office is situate at) __ST. ALBANS ROAD, STAFFORD,__
__STAFFORDSHIRE.__

(hereinafter called 'the Contractor') of the other part. WHEREAS the Employer is desirous of: __4. STOREY OFFICE BLOCK.__

(hereinafter called 'the Works') at __NORTHFIELDS, KIDSGROVE.__
__STAFFORDSHIRE.__

and has caused Drawings and Bills of Quantities showing and describing the work to be done to be prepared by or under the direction of __R.G. PICKERING, DIPL. ARCH. A.R.I.B.A.__
of __THE ENGLISH ELECTRIC CO. LTD.,__
__DICK KERR WORKS, STRAND ROAD, PRESTON. LANCS.__ his Architect

2   The Employer will pay to the Contractor the sum of __Two Hundred & Thirteen Thousand, One Hundred & Eighty Six Pounds, seven shillings & seven pence.__
(£213,186: 7 : 7) (hereinafter referred to as 'the Contract Sum') or such other sum as shall

32

Above : An early Low Voltage Motor Control Centre (MCC) which was the mainstay of the LV Division for many decades. Essentially the MCC provided fuse protected and metered distribution outlets with some limited sequence control for three phase motors in a factory

TYPE ZDS2

VARIABLE SPEED D.C. DRIVE

NOMINAL 14 H.P.—400/440 VOLT 50 CYCLE SUPPLY

STANDARD SPECIFICATION

INPUT   400/440 volts 50 cycles three phase.

OUTPUT   Nominal 14 H.P. Constant Torque Drive. Speed Range 20 : 1 continuously variable. Speed Regulation within 4% of top speed at any pre-set speed within the speed range, irrespective of load applied.

Above figures assume a constant voltage supply with motor running at normal working temperature.

MOTOR   'English Electric' 14 H.P. Stability Compound Wound D.C. Motor.

Speed range, frame size and mounting to suit application.

CONTROLLER
Dimensions: Length 2' 6"
    Width 2' 0"
    Height 4' 6"
Weight: Approx. 10½ cwt.

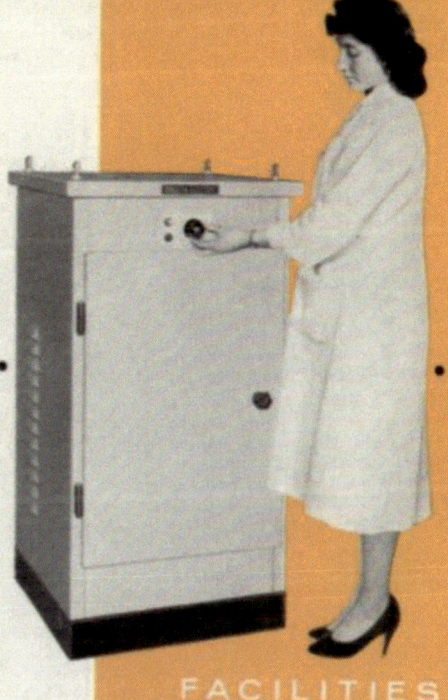

FACILITIES

STANDARD

Uni-directional local speed control
Start/Stop push-button operation
Inherent field failure protection
Adjustable current limit protection

OPTIONAL

Bi-directional control
Remote control
Tension control
Inching
Input voltage and frequency other than standard
Speed regulation better than standard
Compensation for mains variation
Ambient rating higher than standard
Interlocked mains isolation switch
Sustained overload protection

'ENGLISH ELECTRIC'

Control Gear Division · Kidsgrove · Stoke-on-Trent

WORKS: STAFFORD · PRESTON · RUGBY · BRADFORD · LIVERPOOL · ACCRINGTON

Publication ES/206   Printed in England

Brochure from the 1960s Showing a 14 Horse Power Variable Speed DC Drive Unit Modelled above by Kath Bossons (nee Dutton) a production assembler

THE ENGLISH ELECTRIC COMPANY LIMITED

TELEPHONE KIDSGROVE 3511
CABLES ENELECTICO STOKE-ON-TRENT

TELEX 36125
TELEGRAMS ENELECTICO STOKE-ON-TRENT TELEX

KIDSGROVE   STOKE-ON-TRENT   STAFFS.

A. C. Hall, Esq.,
13 Coronation Avenue,
Alsager,
Stoke-on-Trent.

OUR REF   TWD/JF
TELEPHONE EXTENSION No. 675
YOUR REF

3rd October, 1969.

Dear Mr. Hall,

    Further to your recent application for employment with this Company, we are pleased to confirm your appointment as Wireman at our Kidsgrove Works at a commencing rate of pay of 300/-d. (three hundred shillings only), plus bonus as discussed, per 40 hour week as from Monday, 6th October, 1969.

    Your normal hours of work will be 8.00 a.m. - 4.30 p.m. Monday to Friday inclusive, with half an hour for lunch, making a total of 40 hours for a normal working week.

    Would you please report to C13 Section at 8.00 a.m. on 6th October, to commence your duties.

    May we take this opportunity of wishing you a long and happy period of employment with our Company.

                            Yours faithfully,
for: THE ENGLISH ELECTRIC COMPANY LIMITED

T. W. Dawe
PERSONNEL OFFICER

Employment offer letter to Clive Hall as wireman starting in October 1969 at an impressive £15 (300 shillings) per week. Clive remained at Kidsgrove until his retirement in 1987. It is interesting to note that Kidsgrove was still using the English Electric name even though it had become GEC the previous year. Also of note is the old telephone number Kidsgrove 3511 and the use of Telex and Telegram details in the header - this was before the Fax machine came into use.

The Transistor Age

During the 1960's transistor circuits became increasingly popular and printed circuit board production began in earnest at Kidsgrove. Transistors started to take the place of valves, relays and electromechanical sequencers. The expertise in logic circuits developed by the computer division could be migrated to the control gear division and by the mid 1960's the NORLOG range of logic blocks was in widespread use. Each NORLOG block contained transistors, diodes and resistors and carried out basic computer logic functions such as AND and OR gates and FLIP-FLOPS. The key engineer responsible for this work was Tony Danbury.

At the heart of any analogue control system is a device known as an Operational Amplifier (Op Amp). English Electric set about designing a range of standard Op Amp circuits but not as one would expect at Kidsgrove works! The Kidsgrove works was becoming overcrowded and around 1964 they rented out an old mill in Newcastle Under Lyme on the A34. This was called Cross Heath Works and still exists today as "Swift House" – now a motorcycle shop. The first Op Amp was called DCA1 which was soon followed by DCA2. This was about 4 inches square and is shown below.

DCA2 Operational Amplifier circa 1964

As control systems became more complicated, a smaller solution was needed and the development team at Cross Heath went on to produce units about 1.5 inches long such as the CA4 (below). All the components were now housed in a small plastic case and was the forerunner of todays integrated circuit Op Amps.

The key development engineer who pioneered this work was Tony Luffman. On his team were others including Bill Chadwick who went on to become a key design engineer at Kidsgrove when Cross Heath works was closed. The Op Amp modules were fitted to standard size circuit boards which in turn were fitted into a subrack or 'bin'. This system was called UNISTAT and provided the control functions in Automatic Voltage Regulators (AVRs) and in thyristor drive units. This type of modular concept lead to standardisation of the basic system building blocks and reduced engineering costs on contracts.

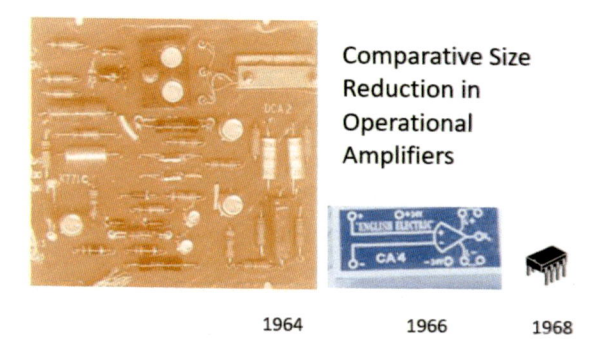

Comparative Size Reduction in Operational Amplifiers

1964   1966   1968

Although the concept of the CA range of Op Amps had been made obsolete by the advent of true integrated circuits such as the 702 and 741, they remained in use by English Electric well into the 1970s.

Assembly of control PCBs into "bins" at Cross Heath works - Elaine Wood in foreground

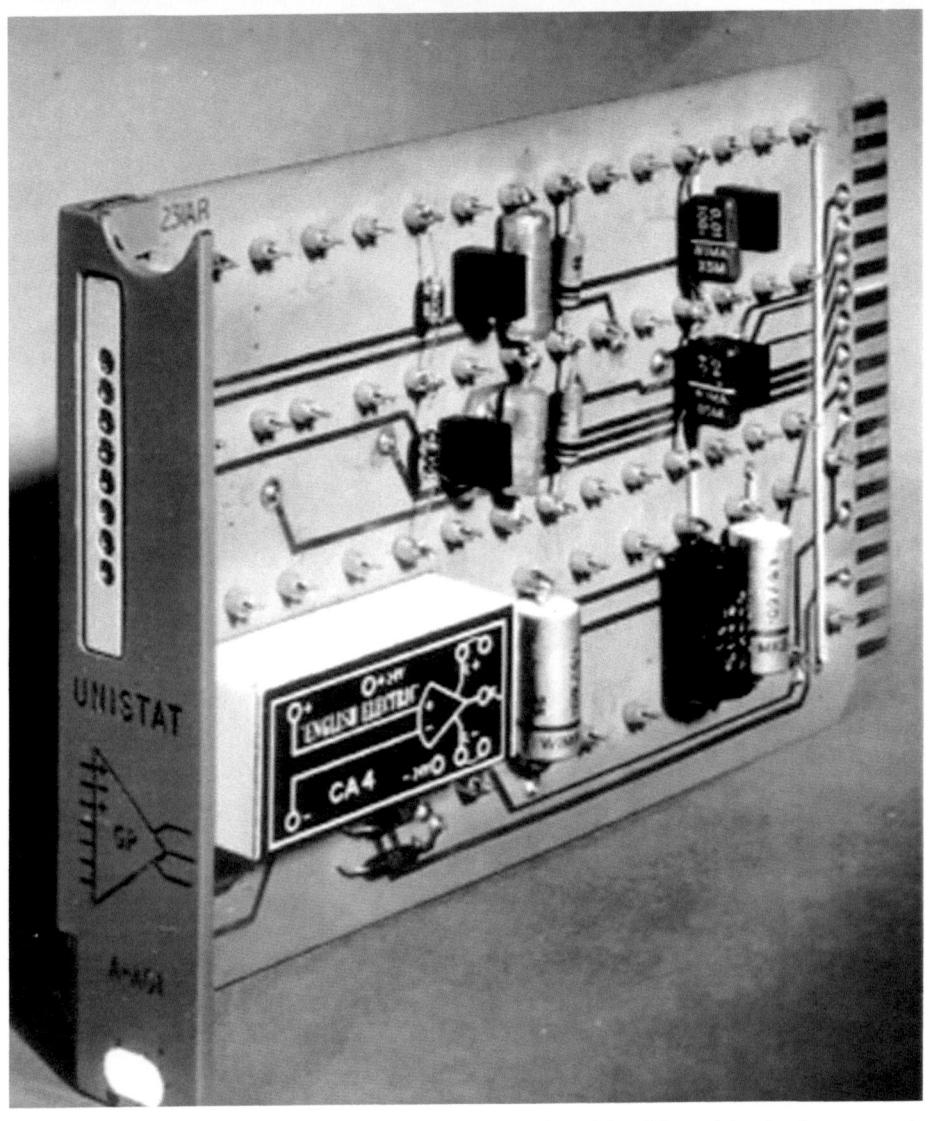

Above: UNISTAT modules provided standardized building blocks for complex control systems

The Price of Electronics

In the 1960s the price of electronics was very high compared to today. The CA4 Operational Amplifier in 1965 was priced at £9. 10s which represented a weeks wages for some people at the time. Today, similar functions can be achieved with a chip costing under £1 so in real terms around 200 times less expensive allowing for inflation.

Computer History at Kidsgrove

The introduction to the English Electric Employees Handbook from 1970 mentions that the factory-produced computers known as DEUCE and LACE. These names are now long forgotten by many, but what exactly were the first computers like and how did they come about? The first digital computer made at Kidsgrove can be traced back to the days of the Second World War at the code breakers at Bletchley Park

Early Computer Development

Post Office engineer, Tommy Flowers was responsible for developing the world's first electronic computer during world war two. The machine, known as Colossus was used to crack the top-secret German code produced by the Lorenz cipher machine. (Lorenz was a far more advanced version of the famous Enigma cipher machine). At the end of the war the Colossus machine was destroyed on the orders of Winston Churchill. In 1946 the National Physical Laboratory proposed the manufacture of a new computer and a team led by Alan Turing was engaged on its design. The machine would be called ACE - which stood for Automatic Computing Engine.

Following the success of ACE it was realised that reliability and performance could only be enhanced by collaboration with industry. In 1949 the National Physical Laboratory proposed that the English Electric Company was the natural choice for an industrial partner. The new computer project was to be called DEUCE and would be built at Kidsgrove.

The English Electric DEUCE computer

DEUCE stands for "Digital Electronic Universal Computing Engine"

DEUCE had two levels of storage, much as in modern machines. The high-speed storage was a set of mercury delay lines of varying sizes. These are tubes containing mercury, into which a stream of sonic pulses representing each bit is injected by a transducer at one end. A microphone at the other end received the pulses a few milliseconds later, and they were then processed and modified if needed, squared up, and fed back into the transmitting transducer. Data could thus be recycled indefinitely. These delay lines were the forerunner of core memory, which had not yet appeared.

Above : The production line for the sub-assemblies used to make the DEUCE computer. Pam Austin, Eileen Rushton, June Hill and Dora Myatt.

The second storage level was more similar to modern devices - a magnetic drum not unlike a present-day disk. Capacity was less however being 48K 32-bit words - around 200 kb in modern terms.

The other devices were a card reader and a punch. There were no magnetic tapes and all programs were loaded stand-alone from cards.

The machine did not have an operating system in the modern sense. There were two primitive languages; Alphacode and Easicode.

DEUCE Mk1 computer equipment during test and programming at Kidsgrove in the late 1950s. Two men here are identified as Jeremy Walker and Frank Thompson

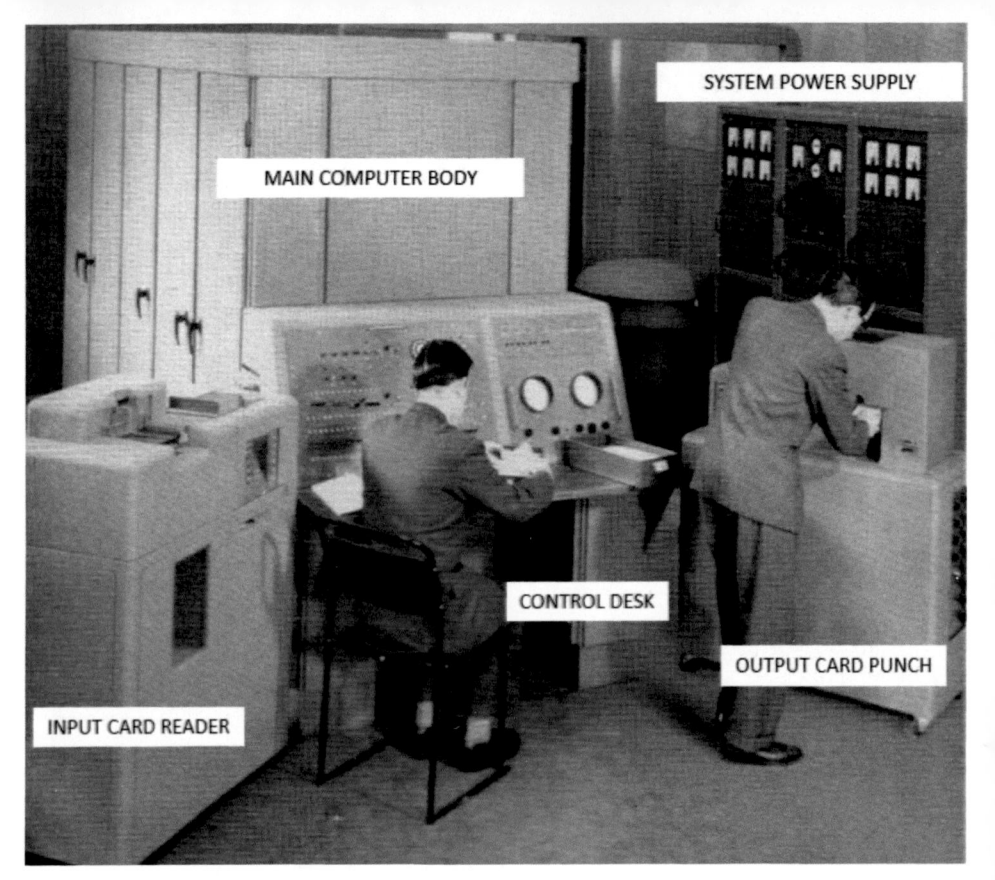

Above : DEUCE computer in operation at Marconi House, London. I have labelled the main parts.

The English Electric KDF9 Computer

The English Electric KDF9 was in use from about 1963 and was regarded as a very successful machine. It was one of the first machines to have a full pre-emptive operating system. It also had floating point capability, using a 48-bit word, which provided good numerical precision. The KDF9 also provided double-length floating point instructions, using 96 bit numbers.

Basic features

The KDF9 had up to 32 kilobytes (not megabytes!) of core memory (made up of real magnetic core). There were no disks; backing storage was provided by magnetic tape units that could be partially rewound and selectively overwritten, provided the programmer was very careful. The operating system, known as "Director" was very sophisticated for its time.

English Electric Computers Made at Kidsgrove

Model	Date of Introduction
LACE	1954
DEUCE 2/2a	1955 - 1957
KDP10 (RCA 501)	Aug 1962
KDN2	Sept 1962
KDF9	Apr 1963
KDF6	Sept 1963
KDF8	Oct 1964
KDF7	1965
System 4/10	Jan 1967
System 4/30	Mar 1967
System 4/50	Sept 1967
System 4/70	Dec 1967
M2112	1968
M2140	1968

The manufacture of high speed line printers - English Electric, Kidsgrove in 1968.

This would be on the Westfields side

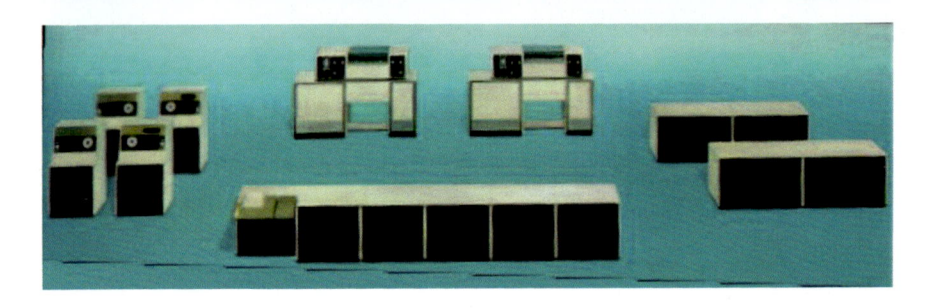

Above - full system M2140 - capacity of 65k instructions with 15 processors. Joined end to end this computer would be 32 feet long! The same functions can now be housed on a wristwatch.

ENGLISH ELECTRIC

M2140
A low cost multi-processor for computation and control

The M2140 was the last computer made by English Electric. As a part of the Industrial Expansion Act of the Wilson Labour Government, EE was forced to sell off its computer business to form ICL. The objective was to create a British computer industry that could compete with major world manufacturers like IBM

The GEC Era

In the late 1960s, the British electrical industry underwent a revolution as GEC acquired Associated Electrical Industries (AEI) in 1967, which encompassed Metropolitan-Vickers, BTH, Edison Swan, Siemens Bros., Hotpoint and W.T. Henley. Then in 1968, GEC merged with English Electric, incorporating Elliott Bros., The Marconi Company, Ruston and Hornsby, Stephenson, Hawthorn & Vulcan Foundry, Willans and Robinson and Dick Kerr. The era of English Electric was over and the new era as GEC began. Sir Arnold Weinstock was Managing Director and Lord Nelson was Chairman. The new company was called GEC-Elliot Automation Ltd and Kidsgrove was GEC-Elliot Industrial Controls Division. The GEC era represented the longest period of stability for the company and would last for 21 years. At the same time as the merger the computer part of the company (English Electric Leo-Marconi Computers) was sold off to become International Computers Ltd or ICL.

Stability and Steady Growth - The 1970's

With the coming of the 1970's the company laid the foundations that were establish a stable period that would last for more than 20 years.

Two men set the company direction for this period - Mr Don Prowse as Managing Director and Mr John Nixon as Director and General Manager.

The company established itself into product divisions:

* Low Voltage Motor Control Centres
* Drives and Machine Tool Products
* Drives Systems
* Standard Control Products

Each of these trading divisions shared the common resources of the factory such as Assembly and Wiring, Printed Circuit Boards, Coilwinding, the Paint Shop and so forth. The Quality Control Department employed nearly 200 inspectors and testers and was an independent function reporting to the General Manager.

Above: Northfields Office Block showing the bus stops which brought in most of the workforce from Stoke on Trent and South Cheshire. The factory Main Works is visible in the background

Northfields Office Block was the heart of design engineering and commercial operations for the company.

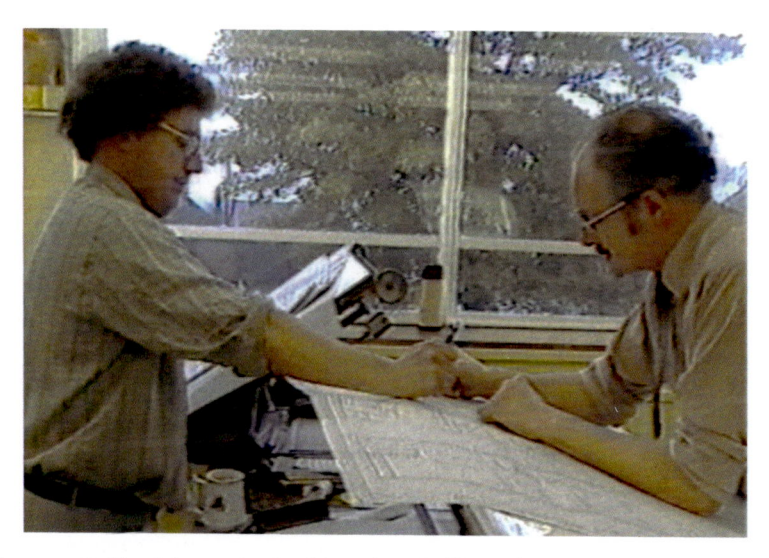

John Grocott & Fred Jones in the Drawing Office which was paper based up until CAD in the mid 1980s

The ground floor started with a large reception area and behind that were fax/telex offices plus the typing pool. Opposite to these were the customer training rooms for drives and GEM80 training which were set up in the 1980s. Towards the end of the block were the director's offices.

The functions of the upper floors varied over Northfields long existence but would generally contain the engineering and commercial functions for the divisions including Drives Products, Drives Systems, Low Voltage Control Gear, GEM80 Products, GEM80 Applications and Microprocessor Development. The only division not housed in Northfields was that of Standard Control Products who accommodated in the huts.

DC Drives

Thyristor based DC drives dominated Kidsgrove's output in the 1970s and 80s with a range called GEMDRIVE. They featured a hinged cover or gate, a metal chassis and blower fans to cool the heatsink mounted thyristors.

At this time the phrase BDM – or Basic Drive Module was coined which remained in use thereafter. The GEMDRIVE range went from around 11kW to 110kW in this BDM form. In the smaller drives there were two PCBs – one for the control circuits and another for the interfacing to the thyristors which contained filtering circuity known as "snubbers". All the control was done via Operational Amplifiers with only minor use of digital logic.

At the top end of the range was the "Anti-Parallel" GEMDRIVE which contained two, three phase thyristor bridges with powerful control functions. The image below gives an idea of how complicated the control electronics had become with provision for extra PCBs mounted on the gate. This was the Rolls Royce of DC drives. On the downside, assembly time for the PCBs and the unit was lengthy and there was a lot of set up and testing of the final product making it expensive to produce.

GEMDRIVE MICRO

The logical progression for the DC drives was the introduction of microprocessors which occurred with the introduction of the GEMDRIVE MICRO in 1984. This was the first digital DC drive and featured programmable parameters that were stored in EEPROMs. The drive could also communicate directly with the GEM80 which was the company's own make PLC.

DC Drives Systems

As well as selling drives as products, Kidsgrove also provided complete drive systems. A drive system would provide full operational control of all the motors on a customer's production line. The key application was in metals such as steel rolling and finishing mills but many other industries were covered such as cable making and tyre production. The strategy for Drives Systems was to have a standard "base" drive cubicle which could then be tweaked to suit the specific application. One such range was called GEMPACK. Many units – as pictured below – would form a long suite of cubicles and all motor sizes could be accommodated.

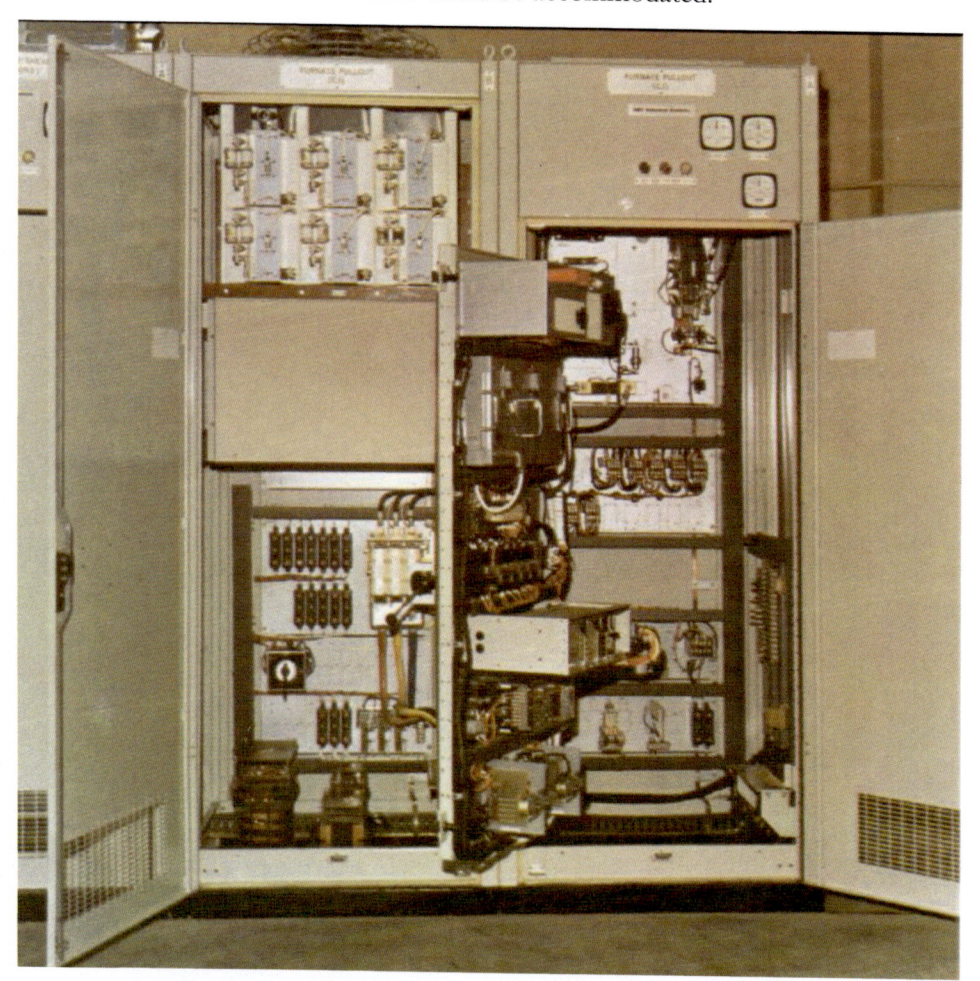

GEMPACK – The Platform for High Power Drive Systems

The GEMPACK design featured a main thyristor power bridge for armature control (top left in the cubicle picture) which was controlled via a T123 Firing Circuit panel fitted on a swinging gate. There was also a field control unit.

The regulator controls were provided by a range of PCBs called the A700 Series which had evolved from the UNISTAT modules covered earlier. The number and type of these modules would vary to suit the application.

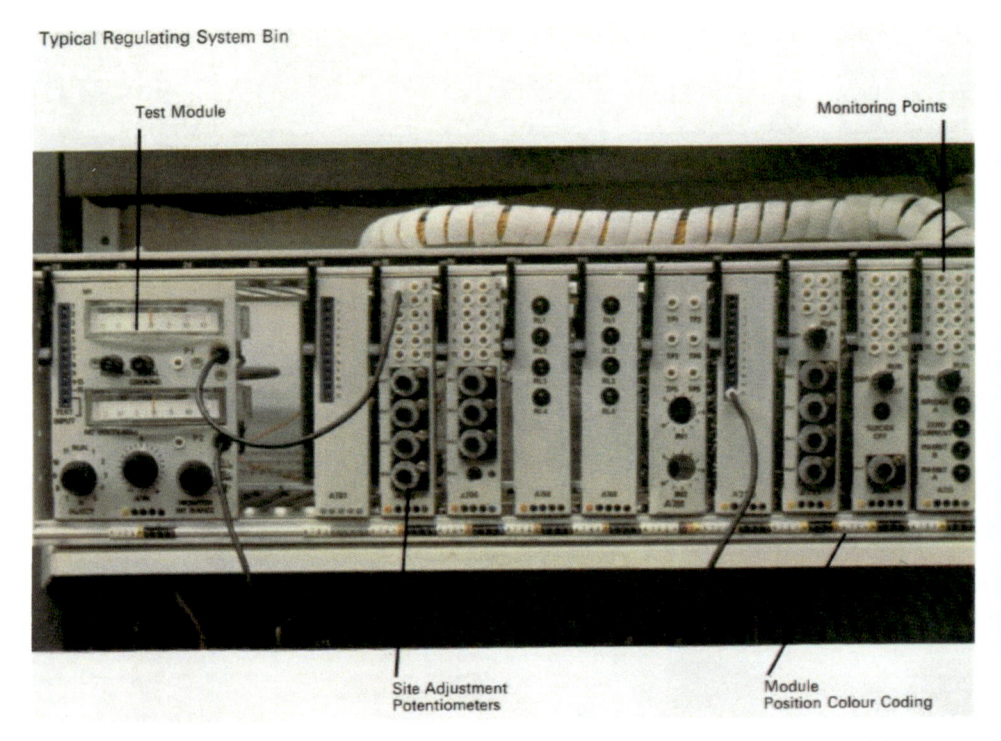

Typical Regulating System Bin

Test Module — Monitoring Points

Site Adjustment Potentiometers — Module Position Colour Coding

The Drive Systems business provided high value projects for Kidsgrove with values typically from £100k to over £1M.

George Taylor was a contracts engineer at Kidsgrove for many years and provides the following account. Of particular note is the representative list of contracts undertaken.

"From 1969 to 1972, I was a Senior Contracts Engineer with D J Watson, Contracts Manager and S T Mayfield, the Commercial Manager, at GEC-Elliott Industrial Controls Division. The majority of the work was on contracts for thyristor drive and processor systems for Rugby Projects. In addition to the thyristor drives, M2140, M2110/12, Datapac, Norlog and Unistat was the other equipment used.

One project from this period remembered well was a computer system for ICI Research at Pangbourne on the Thames. The equipment was an ICL System 4/70 mainframe computer working with a GEC M2140 industrial processor, the first time this was done. The two had to work and communicate for 24 hours under defined conditions to prove the newly developed software in order to be accepted.

Changes at GEC led to an offer of a post at Leicester which was rejected. Obliged to accept redundancy, I worked abroad and in North Yorkshire before returning to GEC in 1978. Through contacts, I was recruited by John Higginson, Division Manager of the Drive Systems Division, to work as a Senior Contracts Engineer in conjunction with Derek Mack, Project Manager, on the hoped for £1M order for GEC equipment for the Thames Board board making mill at Workington, which materialised. The mill, now owned by Iggesund, upgraded, is still operating.

An enjoyable 13 years was then spent at Kidsgrove, working first with Derek, then with Jim Sharp, Section Leader, contract managing a wide range of orders for Gemdrive thyristors controllers, LV, GEM80, motors, cabling and commissioning. Jim managed most of the contracts for steelworks. Other Contract Engineers were John Swann, Sam Millington and Bill Eccles, Contract Manager was Brian Noonan. Although offered a new position in 1991, I left as I was unsettled by the proposed future management structure and the risk of redundancy.

The enjoyable aspect of the work was co-operation with the Design Engineers, managed by Richard `Dick' Hammond, and personnel from all the other departments, customers and suppliers. I recall the names of many of the engineers, John Peet, Derek Griffiths, Paul Davies, Pat Knight, Phil Martin, Don Gilbert, Gerry Chapman, Naj Sohal, Andy Rhodes, Bob Leeming, Frank Griffiths, Alan Price, and Jim Valentine. Many worked on the contracts listed below. As light relief, when a penalty/fixed delivery date contract was delivered on time and in recognition of the effort involved, we had a small celebration in the canteen.

A very small sample list of significant contracts handled by the division is listed below:

Date	Value	Customer	Equipment	Product/output/purpose
1978	£1.5M	Thames Board Mills	Mill, Workington	Cardboard manufacture
1979	£66K	RCSL for Maspio Cement	Aerial Ropeway, Atbara, Sudan	Limestone transport across N Then world's longest at 13mi
1978/9	£146k	Stamco UK for IMI	1000/650mm Slitting Lines	Metals
1980	£133k	Michelin, Stoke	Rubber processing plant	Large tyre making
1981	£131k	AEI Cables, Gravesend	Cable making plant	Electrical cables - World first use a computer instead of gearboxes for set up
1982/6	£1.5M	STC Southampton	Fibre optic cable plant	Cable for a section of the firs Fibre Optic Transatlantic cab others
1986	£328k	Thomas Bolton, Froghall	Cross Country Mill Drive	Copper rolling
1987	£200k	Markham for Dover Harbour	Hoist equipment	Roll on Roll off Ferry
1987	£739k	BSC Ravenscraig	5000HP Reversing Rougher	Steel rolling
1988	£242k	BS Ebbw Vale	Electro-plating mill	Tin plating of steel she
1988	£124k	C&P Sidmar, Belgium	Skip hoist	Steelworks blast furnac
1989/90	£1.67M	BS Orb, Newport, Gwent	Rolling mills	Line modernisation

One recollection from 1969 was an event at ICL. A very large screen was installed in reception showing daily the position of all the yachts in the first Sunday Times Golden Globe Round the World single handed yacht race. This was the race where a Donald Crowhurst committed suicide in the Atlantic, having falsified his positions to imply that he was leading when he wasn't."

Below: Ron Huxley, Frank Danby, Mick Bailey wiring up of AVR panels in the main bays, 1970's

Southfields

The Southfields factory building provided feeder services such as sheet metal for the computer business. With the formation of ICL as a separate company in 1968 these functions were moved across the road leaving Southfields empty. In 1973 GEC Radio and Television moved from the main bays into Southfields factory and offices. There they produced radios, music centres such as the 5020 and a wide range of other products including Red Ring showers and controllers for pelican crossings. In 1978 Radio and TV closed down and shortly after GEC-Marconi Space and Defence Systems occupied Southfields building. Security for the site was tightened up due to the nature of the defence contracts. round this time the "Elliot" part of the name was dropped and the company became GEC Industrial Controls.

External & Internal Views of GEC Marconi, Southfields Building with Mow Cop on the Horizon at the top

1980

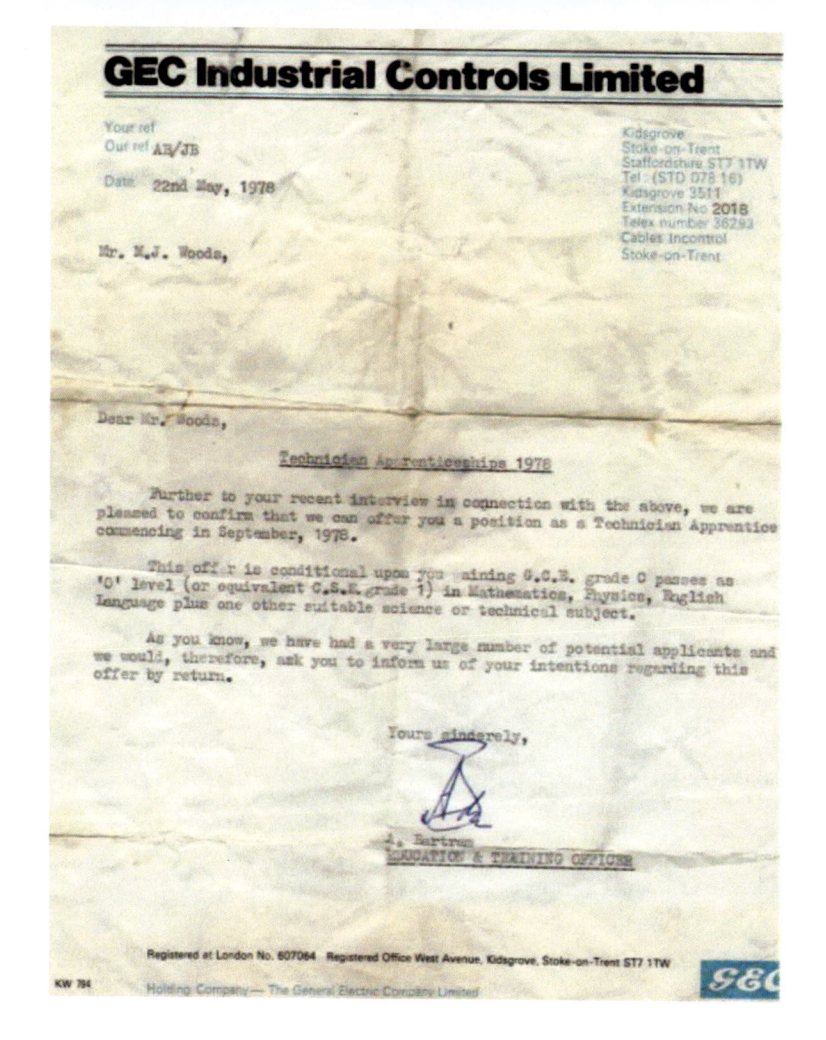

The author's Offer Letter to Join Kidsgrove as Technician Apprentice 1978

In the foreground can be seen the huge office block of ICL. Across West Avenue is the Southfields Factory and Offices of GEC

Originally many firms were involved in specifying a common approach to electronics for all of GEC including GEC Computers, Process Control Leicester and Process Instruments Lewisham. They all pulled out leaving Kidsgrove and Rugby to complete the project which lead to GEM80.

SOLIEE Project

In the 1970s, GEC decided to produce common standards for all light electronic equipment. The exercise was known as SOLIEE, Standardisation of Light Industrial Electronic Equipment. Its aim was for GEC Process Instruments, GEC Process Automation, GEC Electrical Projects, and GEC Industrial Controls to all use the same standard sizes of PCBs and subracks and connectors, etc., so that equipment designed by these different GEC companies, when supplied on the same contract, would all look the same, even though the detail design would be by different companies. It also involved part of Process Instruments in France (long before Alsthom mergers were thought of), and some meetings were held in Stanhope Gate to make it easier for the French guys to attend. It was when Process Automation and Process Instruments dropped out of SOLIEE that Projects and Industrial Controls went ahead with developing the GEM80 PLC. Note also that Process Automation already marketed a rather simple PLC where the program was burnt into fused memory chips (not even re-programmable like EPROMs).

Pictured above is a group photo taken in the Director's Dining room of the canteen block on the retirement of the Chairman Mr. C.P. Holder. Central in the picture is Mrs June Cross who was the secretary to the M.D. for many years. Also of note here is Mr. C.G. Burcher (#19) who was Director and General Manager immediately prior to the arrival of John Nixon.

1.	*Mr. K.A. Hall, Export Sales Manager	14.	Mr. C.H. Jones, Financial Controller
2.	Dr. D.G. Leese, Company Doctor, Kidsgrove	15.	Mr. C.G. Burcher, Director and General Manager
3.	Mr. I.G. Hirst, Works Manager, Kidsgrove	16.	*Mr. D.W. Prowse, Engineering Director and General Manager, Metal Industries & Mining Divisions, Electrical Projects
4.	*Mr. J.A. Rudge, Commercial Director		
5.	*Mr. W.D. Sinclair, Director Technical Services	17.	*Mr. G.P. Jansen, Managing Director
6.	*Mr. T.H. McLellan, Publicity Manager	18.	*Mr. E.J. Bowers, Finance Director
7.	*Mr. D.R. Fricker, Engineering Standards Manager	19.	Mr. C.P. Holder, Ex-Chairman, now retired
8.	Mr. I.R. Smith, Company Contracts Manager	20.	Mrs. J. Cross, Secretary to Managing Director, Kidsgrove
9.	Mr. R. Padgett, Site Services Manager, Kidsgrove	21.	Mr. P.R. Gogerly, Marketing Manager
10.	Mr. R.L. McNaughton, Chief Engineer, Kidsgrove	22.	Mr. D.L. Hunt, Engineering Manager, Rugby
11.	*Mr. J.L. Russell, Sales Director and General Manager, General Industries & Marine Divisions, Electrical Projects	23.	Mr. G. Sanders, Personnel Manager, Kidsgrove
12.	Mr. A.G. Jutton, Licensing Manager		Unless otherwise indicated, individuals are responsible for GEC Industrial Controls Limited.
13.	Mr. I.A. Ferguson, Materials Management Manager, Electrical Project		*Indicates responsible for GEC Electrical Projects Limited as well as GEC Industrial Controls Limited.

The Microprocessor Revolution 1980's & GEM80

The decade of the 80's was dominated by the widespread application of microprocessors and in particular GEM80. GEM80 was a range of Programmable Logic Controllers (PLCs) powered by the INTEL range of microprocessors such as the 8085. It was a joint development between Kidsgrove and Rugby and at it's launch in May 1979 was years ahead of the competition. It had built in serial communications and an integral video graphics system. GEM80's success was down to first class hardware, user friendly software with built in special functions combined with dynamic marketing from the new management team of Brian Pope (Division Manager) and Berkeley Fenn (Product Manager). Pope and Fenn took the GEM80 into all industrial sectors including the motor industry (Ford, Leyland, etc), Petrochemicals, Steel making, food (Cadburys) and great inroads were made into export markets both in Europe and the USA. To illustrate the rise of GEM80 sales went from virtually zero in 1979 to more than £8M by 1984! These sales rivalled the traditional activities of LV and Drives. At the end of the decade total sales for GEC Kidsgrove were £65 million with 1,400 people employed.

Brian Pope - GEM80 Divisional Manger

Berkeley Fenn - GEM80 Product Manager

The photo on the next page shows the GEM80-200 series controller which was mounted in a 19" subrack. Optional modules could be fitted such as analogue input and output boards, serial communications, etc.

Major Investment and New Technology in the 1980's

The first half of the 80's saw the microprocessor being put to use in other products.

In 1984 the GEMDRIVE MICRO was introduced which was the company's first processor based DC drive offering full digital control and serial communications. Even Standard Control Products got in on the act with the introduction of the MICROGEM small PLC in 1985 that was sold in the same way as push buttons and lamps. The year of 1984 represented a major investment period for the company with capital spend running into several millions. In February the Computer Aided Design room came on line in the ground floor of Northfields building. In December 1984 the company set up the Hybrid Circuits manufacturing plant (at the back of the canteen block).

This facility produced miniature circuit modules to be used on a variety of drives and PLC boards. The area was used the concept of clean rooms and operators wore full overalls, hats, etc to exclude dust. Steve Beattie and Gary Jones ran the plant. 1984 also saw the first real progress with the new surface mount technology that is now standard for PCBs. The first board to benefit from this was the MPR2 protection relay - an SCP product.

PCB Manufacture was a Key Part of the Company

Tony Leake (bottom left) was a Production Engineer who started as an Apprentice at the same time as the Author

Training and Development

Following the installation of the new hybrid facility in the canteen block the training department was re-located to mezzanine floor at the north end of Bay 1 in the main works. The training department was run by Peter Errett with Alan Bartram as Education and Training Officer and Ted Tomkins as Instructor.

The company had a long tradition of recruitment and development of young people. Each year around a dozen technician apprentices would be recruited from local schools and would go on to HNC/HND courses. The practical aspects of the training were regulated by the Engineering Industry Training Board or EITB. Many of these technicians would go on to become senior managers and engineers within the company such as Norman Stubbs and Ken Walters (Division Managers of Drives and LV respectively).

Undergraduates were sponsored by GEC and spent vacation periods undergoing practical training. Graduates were recruited from the University 'milk round' and would provide the foundations for future development and applications engineers. The company purchased Newcroft House near the works in 1981 to use as student accommodation. The 1980s saw the establishment of the Youth Training Scheme (YTS) by the government. Around ten YTS trainees were set on each year and trained for clerical and technical careers. This meant that at any one time around 70 trainees were 'on the books' ensuring that future vacancies could be easily filled by trained people.

The company also provided training and development for the rest of the workforce both by in house courses and lectures and by providing funding for college courses.

Many people attended customised courses at the GEC Management College at Dunchurch near Rugby. At the start of the eighties George Taylor took over from Jeff Tether as Personnel Manager. After he retired a few years later he was replaced by Neil Roberts. During this time Ted Johnson was Assistant Personnel Manager. The later half of the eighties decade saw several key changes in the company. Brian Pope - Divisional Manager GEM80 moved to EMICC in Detroit to promote GEM80 in the USA and Canada. David Slingsby took over the Division. In March 1985 the company, in association with Simon Carves Ltd, signed the Yerevan Contract. This was the biggest contract that the company had won with and involved the building of a new factory in Yerevan, Armenia to manufacture GEM80 products for the Soviet market. A new Division was created for this originally managed by Alan Jutton. Yet another new Division was created in 1988. It was called CAPS - Control and Process Automation - and provided systems engineering for GEM80 projects such as paint plants at Fords and Steel making in Sidmar, Belgium. Derek Spencer managed CAPS Division.

Brian Pope, Divisional Manager GEM80 explains the new customer training facilities to Lord Nelson (son of George Nelson). Pictured also are Janet Hill, Software Engineer and instructors Mark Woods and John Hughes

Service Functions in the 70s - 80's

Reception, Telephones, Telex and Fax

The main reception was in Northfields Office block and immediately behind that was the telex/Fax room which had about four women working there. At one point there was a second reception in Southfields. The telephone exchange was located above the north end of Bay 1 on a mezzanine floor. Some seven women operated this traditional telephone exchange and pictured below from left to right are Helen Fitton, Pat Statham, Sue Taylor, Janet Wythenshaw and Elaine Carter. Not shown are Nora Smith (supervisor) and Barbara John. The actual mechanical relay room was located in a room below the exchange. All incoming calls would go via this exchange with the operators then putting callers through using the plug boards. People wishing to phone out would need to call the operator and then request an outside line. During the mid-1980s, the old exchange was replaced by a modern, electronic one – the GPT ISLX 1500 made by GEC Plessy Telecom at Coventry. A new plant room was built on the side of the personnel block to house the new cabinets which contained the microprocessor based boards of the ISLX system.

Maintenance

In order to keep the vast site running the company had a large maintenance department that was virtually self-sufficient. The works engineer was Geoff Shenton and under him were various foreman and charge-hands for the different functions such as electricians and mechanical fitters. Geoff had engineered and implemented most of the major site moves and expansion from the late 1950s right up to the mid 1990s.

The following functions existed in maintenance:- electrical workshops, mechanical workshops including a machine shop and welding area, a joinery department, a team of painters and the works garage. The maintenance department purchased its own materials and had a vast store of spare parts. It also maintained its own drawings and technical specifications via the Technical Clerk (Tony Stanyer). In order to look after the 34 acre grounds the company even had three small tractor-mowers at one period for cutting the grass on the sports fields!

Mail Room

At its height there were four full time staff in the mailroom. These were the days before e-mail and faxes had not been out for too long. Therefore written, paper communication was all-important and a vast amount of letters and memos had to be delivered and collected to all sections each day. Mail staff started early in order to have letters available at the start of work. The mailroom staff included John Jones, John Neild, Bill Lally and Tom Smith.

Works Medical Facilities

Like all big companies of the day, Kidsgrove had a works surgery in the basement with a permanent nurse and a visiting doctor – Phillip Leese. Over the canteen block was a works dentist.

Canteen

During the 1980's the canteen was catering for over 1000 people in shifts. In addition to the main areas there were also a number of specialist dining rooms. Managers could eat in the Blue Room with a waitress service, the Directors had their own dining room and there was also a Visitor's Dining Room which was used for entertaining the many customers that were visiting Kidsgrove. Linda Daley was the manager of the canteen during this period. The canteen was also responsible for looking after the many food vending machines on site and also provided a 'toast round' in the mornings.

Documents

The company generated and used tens of thousands of documents each year. Letters, memos, reports and similar documents were produced in the Typing Pool ran by Mary Walton. The typing Pool originally used mechanical typewriters and carbon paper for copies. In the late 1970's specialist electronic word processors were purchased (made by Wang). By 1990 - due to the introduction of the office PC - the services of the Typing Pool were no longer required and the function closed. For many years the company's typewriters were serviced by the local firm OES based in Tunstall which made weekly service visits to the firms 90+ machines. Again, the growth of PCs eventually replaced all typewriters and OES are no longer in business. More technical documentation was produced by the Technical Manuals section, part of the Standards Department (Manager Denis Fricker with Dave Rowley as Head of Standards) which included such functions as Graphic Design and the company library which employed a full time librarian.

The Works Garage

The company has always operated its own works garage from the 1950's. The main aim of the garage was to service and repair the works cars and vans but garage staff also acted as chauffeurs when required. In the 1960's Mr George Hackney was the Transport Manager for English Electric and Fred Crowther was the Garage Foreman. David Buckley joined GEC in 1972 as a motor mechanic followed a year later by Dave Carter as Apprentice Mechanic. In 1980 Fred Crowther retired and his son, Graham Crowther took over. During the 1980's the garage was very busy servicing the cars of both Cegelec and GEC-Alsthom as well as continuing with chauffeuring duties, valeting and so on. In 1992 major redundancies were announced and it was decided that the company could no

Works Garage – Bay 1 Basement - 1955

longer afford its own garage and mechanics. The garage staff were made redundant but David Buckley and Dave Carter were given the chance of setting up as a private garage using the same premises and facilities.

They accepted this offer and Eastfield Garage was born. Being a private firm Eastfield could now service private as well as company vehicles. This situation continued until 2001 and the garage prospered as they took on more and more private customers. By 2001 the works land and buildings now belonged to a separate property division of the parent company. New rent and leasing conditions were proposed that were not acceptable to Eastfield. As a result Eastfield Garage closed in mid-April 2001.

The End of the Decade and the End of GEC at Kidsgrove

1989 marked the start of the biggest series of changes to effect the site since 1968. It was announced that a new company would be formed which was jointly owned by GEC (22%) and the large French company CGE (78%). The new company would be called CEGELEC and would have 27,000 employees world-wide. In December 1989 a new Managing Director took over at Kidsgrove from Don Prowse - Mr John Seed. Seed had come from GEC PIC at New Parks, Leicester and set about to adapt the company to suit its new Anglo-French ownership. At the start of 1990 John Nixon left the company.

Recession, Decline and Downsizing 1990's

Just as the 80's had been the boom years for the company, the 90's were to swing the fully the other way with devastating effects on the workforce.

The UK had started a recession and major companies like steel, mining and the car industry were hitting hard times and not spending. The company's order book fell severely and in May of 1990 some 85 redundancies were announced. Many of the company's senior management lost their jobs as the company re-structured to survive the coming years with a much reduced business level.

Two years later, in 1992, the situation had not improved and at the start of the year a further 90 job losses were announced. As sales continued to fall it became clear that the company could not afford to employ the 1200 people it had. Around March a massive 250 job losses were announced affecting all areas of business. In the second half of 92 another major change was announced. The Low Voltage Control Gear Division and SCP were to be transferred to GEC-Alsthom which had recently been established.

Some 400 people were identified as working in LV or SCP related activities but in the end only 320 were required which lead to a further 95 job losses. By 1993 the Kidsgrove workforce was down to around 700 people - less than half the workforce of 1989.

The reduced numbers on site meant that rationalisation of buildings was needed in order to cut costs. By January of 1993 Northfields office block was finally emptied having been in use for 27 years. Likewise, the old huts were emptied and the original huts A,B,C and D were demolished.

The SCP functions such as coilwinding and assembly moved into Bays 3 and 4 and the Yervan Team (which had been in Huts G and F) moved the Southfields Office block (which had been empty since Marconi closed in 1985).

Electronics manufacturing moved from Bay 5 in the old main works to the new Southfields Factory. Bay 5 was converted to offices for the LV Division (now called GALVE - GEC Alsthom Low Voltage Equipment). The SCP business was moved to GE Liverpool and the coilwinding activity was ceased in favour of bought in transformers. The key words of the decade were "core activities" and everything that was not "core" was to be purchased. Traditional production and quality methods were scrutinised and changed. Full 100% inspection of components was replaced by 'green route' initiatives where the supplier did the checking. Independent inspection was replaced by self-inspection and the test empire was dismantled in favour of test being integrated as part of the production team (or cell).

New Technical Developments

In 1993 a brand new computer system came on line called MFG PRO. This was a totally integrated system that went from order processing right to shipping and invoicing. It replaced many of the separate VAX/IMS systems in use.

The first half of the decade also saw the launch of two new AC drive ranges - the GD2000 and GD4000 products.

1999 The End of LV Manufacture at Kidsgrove

In 1999, GE Alsthom decided to close the LV business which meant the end of production in the Main Bays after some 46 years. This was a very sad occasion resulting in many job losses. Some staff re-located to Manchester but they were in the minority.

The workforce posed for one last photograph shown below.

The Kidsgrove Works in 2000

In 1999 Cegelec had become part of ALSTOM - a new company listed on the stock market that included most of the old Cegelec companies and some of the GEC-Alsthom companies. Further job losses in 1999 had reduced the ALSTOM workforce to 186 people with a turnover of around £14M based in the Southfields building.

By 2000 part of the main bays had been leased to a pharmaceutical distributor and the canteen block was being emptied ready for partial occupation by a Diamond Electronics Ltd. Northfields, N Block and the remains of Huts F-K remained empty.

Across the road ICL had changed from being a computer company to a sub-contract electronics manufacturer first as D2D and then as Celestica. The company prospered due to the boom in mobile phones and communications equipment and had a workforce of more than 2,000. At its peak - around 1988 - the total workforce employed on electrical work was nearly 4,000 split between ICL and GEC.

The Years 2002 - 2004

By the middle of 2002 prospects were looking mixed for the companies on the Nelson Industrial Estate. Celestica (ex-ICL) announced poor results and were considering some 500 job losses on top of the ones lost in 2001. However on the other side of West Avenue things were looking good for ALSTOM.

Above: Site Leader Ian Gilmore with the author (centre) and Czech customer Vaclav Rendall, Prague 2004

Two views from about 2000. Top picture shows the south facing end of Southfields office block. Bottom picture is the same view but panned back to show the entire office block and factory at the rear. The old main works is partially visible in the distance and part of the ICL complex can be seen on the left

Above – North facing view of Southfields Office block looking up West Avenue

The drives sales function had returned from Rugby allowing once again the company to offer a complete range of products and services to its customers.

Turnover on the site was in the order of £15M with a healthy contribution to ALSTOM's profit of more than £1.5M each year.

Large drives were being sold around the world from Brazil to the Czech Republic. In particular the company's MV3000 AEM (active energy management) drives were world leaders for their power and voltage ratings.

On the PLC side, 2002 saw the launch of a brand new Programmable Controller - the GEM80-500. This new PLC had been conceived, designed and built at Kidsgrove and continued the 20-year tradition of GEM80 products.

During this time the parent company ALSTOM was in need of cash and the Kidsgrove factory was providing more than its fair share putting it in a strong position. New investments started to be made in the infrastructure such as new carpets, new washroom facilities and a new coat of paint both inside and out. On the production side investments were being considered for new test gear in order for Kidsgrove to meet the expected demand for DELTA power modules resulting from significant new contracts being won in the USA and Europe. The productivity and efficiency rate was now higher than it had ever been. (in the 1980's sales were around £36k/person compared to 2002s figure of £88k/person.)

On a national level the financial news of the time carried tales of the final downfall of the Marconi Company. Marconi had changed it's name from GEC and had seen its shares fall from more than £12 to 2 p. The once mighty GEC had virtually been destroyed. It is somewhat ironic that the same year saw the death of Lord Weinstock who had been at the helm of GEC from the 1960's. He was gone and so was the empire he had built up.

What had happened - in simple terms - was that in the 1990's GEC had sold off all of its heavy engineering capability (transport, power, transmission, etc) to ALSTOM. This left it with telecommunications which then proceeded to hit a severe recession from which it could not recover. During the period 2002 – 2004, Kidsgrove had introduced many new products continuing the tradition of innovation. In particular the 800 & 1000 Amp liquid cooled DELTA power modules for the MV3000 inverter range was to dominate the output of the Kidsgrove factory from now on. Up to 6 of these modules can be connected to form a drive with a power rating up to 4MW at 690VAC. Kidsgrove markets were also changing – with new business from Wind Energy in the shape of 2.3MW and 3.6MW variable speed turbine systems.

The Surface Mount Assembly Line at Kidsgrove. All the Drive Products used PCB's Made in House

CONVERTEAM & THE WIND POWER ERA

The year 2005 marked a major watershed for the Kidsgrove site. Two key events came together to launch a new age of growth and prosperity. Firstly, the ALSTOM era ended when on November 10, 2005 Barclays Private Equity France (BPEF) became its new shareholder of the Power Conversion Group.

Some four months later on March 30, 2006 this new company was renamed Converteam and was the brainchild of Pierre Bastid, a dynamic business leader from France.

Secondly, 2005 marked the rapid upturn in sales of wind turbine power converters to Bonus Energy of Denmark. This was the culmination of a deal established by the late Ian Gilmore who as General Manager of Kidsgrove had secured this new business in renewable energy. This huge increase in business would transform the site and would ultimately take Kidsgrove to the sales levels not seen since the GEC days of the 1980s.

Above : Converteam board, from left to right Pascal Planchon, Pierre Bastid (President of Converteam), Thierry Perennec with Peter Whitworth and Ian Gilmore

Horse Hollow Wind Farm - Texas

The full story of the wind power breakthrough can be found in Appendix 4

November 2007 – A plaque to mark the 1000th wind turbine converter is unveiled at Kidsgrove Southfields block. General Manager Steve Beattie (centre) was joined by local councillors as well as Directors from Rugby HQ. By the time the factory closed, it had shipped over 10,000 wind turbine converters world-wide

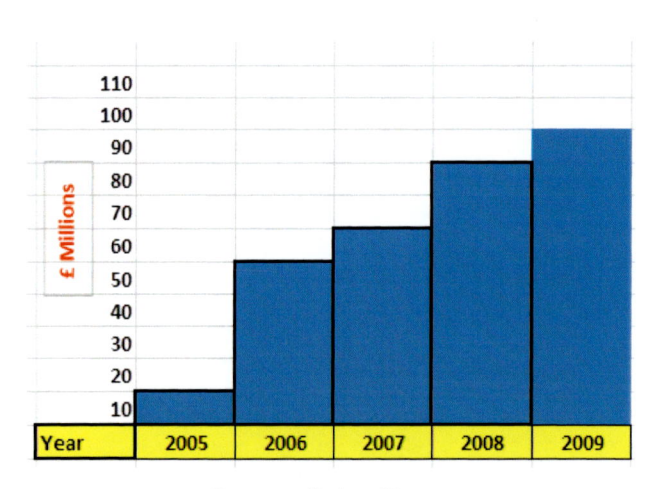

Factory Sales Output

Assembly of early Liquid Cooled Delta Modules at Converteam

The Old Works in Decay 2005-2008

Whilst the Southfields building was becoming fully utilized with wind power products, the rest of the site at the northern end fell into decay. The large main bays of the old works had a eerie emptiness about them and vandalism became rife. The same held true for Northfields office block which had dominated West Avenue since the 1960s.

Top: Bays 1 and 2 of the old main works, May 2005. It had been empty since 1999 when the Low Voltage business (GALVE) moved to Manchester

Lower: Views inside the Northfields Office block 2007

Top: Summer 2008 – only the basement remains after the main works was demolished. This view is looking south with the canteen block in the distance

Lower: The last part remaining of Northfields Office Block with No.1 Gate in the foreground. This part of the site is now a housing estate

The Years 2008 – 2011

The period 2008 – 2011 saw continued growth and profitability at Kidsgrove site which had been called Converteam since 2006. President Pierre Bastid was a frequent visitor to Kidsgrove with his COO Florent Battistella. Both men showed great leadership in transforming the new Converteam group. The Kidsgrove works remained a satellite of the head office at Boughton Road at Rugby and Steve Raynor was the UK Managing Director.

Florent Battistella, 3rd from left, attends a shop floor meeting with Steve Beattie, Joyce Barlow and John Middling, 2008

The output of Kidsgrove was dominated by wind converters which it had been selling to Siemens Wind Power in Denmark since 2005. As these converters represented about 80% of the output, emphasis began to be placed on lean manufacturing and experts were brought in from France to apply techniques which had been developed in the automotive industry. The converter production lines were streamlined with automatic tooling and the throughput of converters peaked at around 40 complete 2.3MW units per week and some 450 Delta power modules. The site moved from a standalone drives and controls company to a mainly manufacturing unit and by this time the traditional functions of applications engineering, tendering, product management, marketing and customer support no longer existed. Design and development engineering continued to exist but with most of its emphasis on the wind converters and power modules. In addition to the lean manufacturing, much attention was placed on the supply chain and cost reduction programmes. The quality function also grew – again mirroring the automotive industry. Some of the key "old" customers remained which were dominated by the drilling firms in Houston Texas. The Texan entrepreneur businessman Kevin Williams had been a great advocate of the Kidsgrove made drive components which he had firmly established in the drilling world providing the workhorse functions of top drives, mud pumps and draw works. The output of converter products into drilling peaked at some £8 million via framework agreements brokered by Williams who also contributed to product development.

Next page shows MV3000 Delta equipment at one of the Texas drilling companies. This is the factory of Oilfield Electric Marine (OEM) which was later sold to LTI.

Above: Top Drive for Oilwell Drilling – using 2100A Liquid Cooled Rectifier and 2 x 1000A Delta Modules

Below: MV3000 Equipment Installed in Containers that are Transported to the Drilling Site

The Kidsgrove factory also supplied products to its fellow Converteam partners. The Glasgow factory made converters for marine applications taking some £3M of product each year.

Converteam units in France, Brazil and North America were also key customers. Around this time, the new market of solar energy emerged with some modest air cooled products going into France and then a major solar expansion by the Pittsburgh factory which took some £8M of liquid cooled power modules for their solar converters. This expansion had been enabled by the creation of a new interface to the Delta power modules which allowed them to be controlled by more powerful PC based Power Electronic Controllers (PECe) instead of the traditional dedicated in Common Drive Controller (CDC) which continued to be used in the traditional markets.

Further expansion of the Kidsgrove portfolio was made possible by Paul Brooks – a dynamic salesman who was always on the lookout for new product and customer opportunities. The first of these was a venture into complete marine converters, starting small at first with a number of Diode Front End (DFE) units for a Denmark marine and offshore firm. Then Brooks negotiated a framework agreement for the supply of Active Front End (AFE) converters for STX of Norway. Two models were designed of 600KW and 1600KW which also incorporated PLC control for system functions and comms. These units were extremely compact.

The other new product stream was the introduction of a medium voltage converter operating at 3.3kV with a power of some 3MW. It was called the MV7303FP as it used flat pack IGBTs instead of the conventional hockey puck compression devices. It was water cooled using a deionized system.

Close to 40 converters were built at Kidsgrove with the biggest contract being for the Vittoria Desalination Plant in Australia which was engineered out of Massy, France.

The converter design was largely done by Kidsgrove engineer Tom Gowans, aided and abetted by Mick Cooper and Paul Challinor.

The MV7303 was a triumph of engineering design for manufacturability and was described as one of the best converters to build by factory assembly staff.

The MV7303, medium voltage drive 3.3kV @ 3MW, some 39 units were made before production was transferred to Glasgow

Semiconductor Supply Crisis and Further Strategy Change

The Converteam international conference in Malta in 2008 was coming to an end when news arrived of the great financial banking crisis marked by the collapse of Lehman Brothers who had filed for bankruptcy. This event marked the start of a global recession which saw many firms go out of business and others to scale back production. One consequence, some 18 months later, was that major manufacturers of the silicon and silicon based devices used in Kidsgrove's power modules cut back output leading to a shortage. This meant that the firm could not fulfil its orders for both wind converters and general product. This event, and others, led to a French director being brought in to run Kidsgrove and the outcome was the decision that all none-wind converter cubicle business should cease. The marine drives were transferred to Glasgow as were the MV7303 medium voltage drives.

2011 CONVERTEAM SOLD TO GENERAL ELECTRIC USA

In March of 2011, General Electric of America announced it was to buy Converteam for $3.2 billion. It had always been the intention of Pierre Bastid to sell the company after increasing its worth nearly eight times since it was bought from ALSTOM. The closing of the sale to GE took place in September of 2011 and was marked by an event at Keele Univeristy where all employees attended and were given a talk by the new boss of Power Conversion Joe Mastrangelo. At this time, Kidsgrove had a new leader – Gary Lynch – who had been in post less than 12 months when GE took over. Gary's title was Director, Renewable Converter Manufacturing, Kidsgrove and he set about modernising the plant. Gary was focused on "process" and introduced many measures to streamline manufacturing which took out cost and improved on time deliveries. Similar measures were taken in the offices as he tried to make the company into a paperless environment. At the corporate level, GE too was into processes and many of the traditional tasks done by secretaries and administrators were converted to online, self-executed "workflows". This included the booking of travel, accommodation, holidays and expense claims. Lynch invested in new office furniture which saw the last of the old desks removed – some of which had started out in English Electric some sixty years before!

2014/15 Demolition, Reconstruction and Investment

Within a few weeks of GE taking over in 2011, they had condemned the old canteen block building which has been used as the company's warehouse. An offsite warehouse was rented which was a few miles away called Rosevale (below) - about 15 minutes away up the A34 towards Newcastle.

Above: The Canteen Block had once housed Directors and Visitors Dining rooms plus the workers canteen under GEC. It became a warehouse in later years before being demolished in 2014

This meant that kitted components had to be delivered many times a day in large lorries hired from transport firm Berser. The old canteen stood idle until 2014 when demolition finally started.

GE had to make up for decades of lack of investment in the site. New energy efficient GE lighting was installed. All the office windows were replaced as were the roofs on the factory and office building. Southfields building was clad and work started on the construction of a new, modern reception to replace what was a little more than a desk under the stairs. By far the biggest investment was the construction of a new warehouse which occupied the site of the old canteen block and was joined on to the existing factory via a tunnel.

October 2015 – the new warehouse is complete

Kidsgrove Works – The End of an Era

On Friday 27th May 2016 it was announced that the GE factory at Kidsgrove was to close with over 240 jobs at risk.

Christmas 2016 was to be the end of 64 years of electronics manufacture on West Avenue. GE, who had owned the business since 2011 announced that they had insufficient work to fill all their factories i.e. too much capacity. The main factory in France had recently moved to modern premises with associated investment and the large facility in Berlin had also benefited from modernisation and investment. Work would be transferred to these other GE locations.

The Demolition of the Southfields Factory and Office Block

In January 2018, work started on the demolition of Southfields. These were the last buildings standing of the original Nelson Industrial Estate.

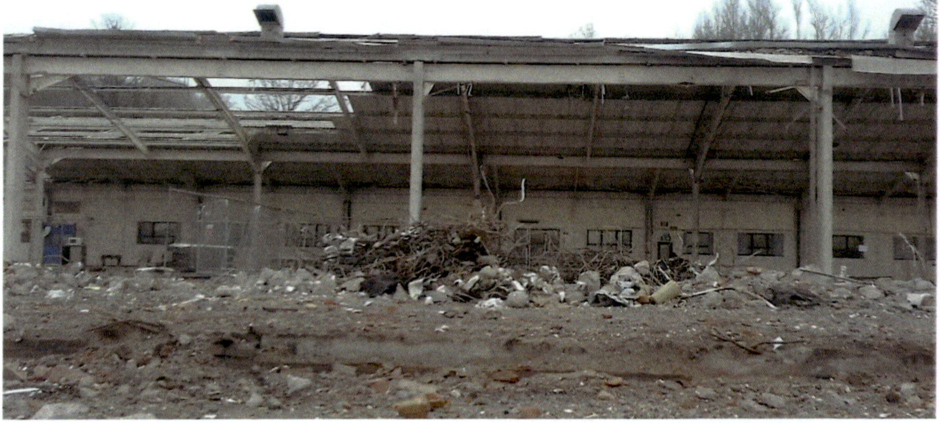

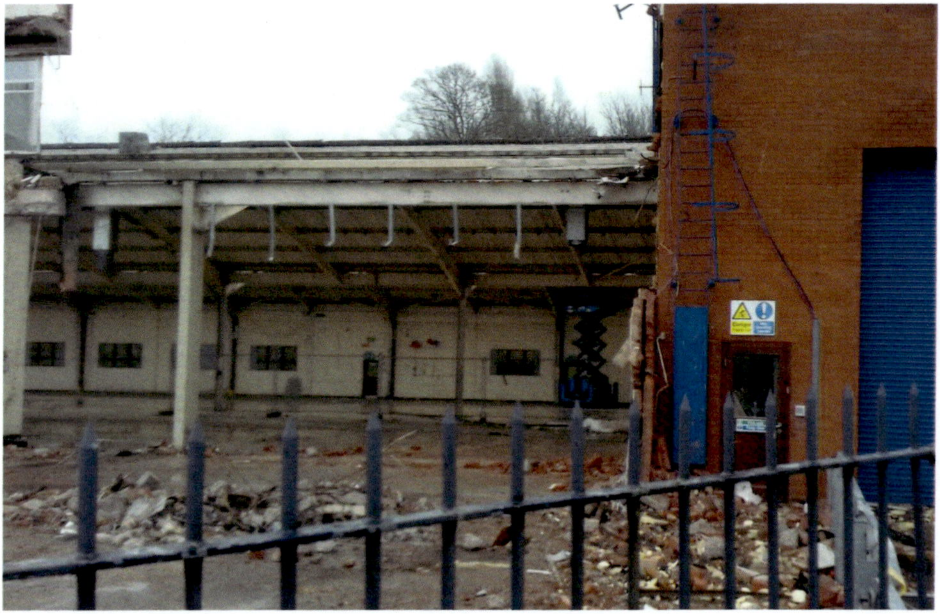

Appendix 1 Timeline

1952	Building work starts on Bays 1 and 2 of the main works
1953	Bays 1 and 2 are occupied and production begins
1954	More land purchased for Westfields and high ground behind bays
1956-9	Bays 4 and 5 constructed
1957-8	Canteen block built
1958-9	Huts A B C and D erected behind Bay 5
1961-6	Canteen block extended
1963	Leo Computers joined EE to become English Electric Leo Computers
1964	Marconi Computers joined EE to become English Electric Leo Marconi Computers
1966	England wins world cup
1966	Northfields Office Block built
1967	GEC acquires AEI group
1968	Plessey attempts takeover of EE (22nd July) causing EE to start talks with GEC.
1968	GEC and English Electric merge (effective 30 Nov 1968) New company at Kidsgrove is initially called English Electric-AEI Industrial Controls
1968	Computer operations separated from EE to form ICL
1969	End of 1969 the name becomes GEC-Elliot
1973	GEC Radio and Television move into Southfields
1978	New Social Club opened by Group MD Mr Jansen in canteen block
1978	GEC Radio and Television closes
1978	Marconi Space and Defence occupies Southfields
1979	GEM80 launched
1984	CAD in Northfields, Hybrids in canteen block
1985	Marconi closes
1989	GEC becomes CEGELEC
1990	Redundancies due to recession 85 people - 2nd May
1992	LV and SCP business transferred to GEC-Alsthom, 90 and then 250 job losses
1993	Northfields Offices emptied
1994	New Dining Room opens in December and old dining room is converted into finished goods store.
1995	Open Day 10th June, Direct Dial In (DDI) phones introduced, 750kW Drives Test Rig installed. Computer Room moved to middle floor from ground floor.
1996	Jan - Alcatel Alsthom buys a third of AEG and the automotive/drives sectors transfers to Cegelec.
1998	October – First Liquid Cooled Delta Power module

1999	May and October - Redundancies, Up to 40 jobs to go as General Drives Division moves to Rugby
1999	Company changes to ALSTOM
1999	December - LV Business moves to Manchester - Main Factory empty
2001	30th March - closure of canteen facility.
2001	20th April - closure of Eastfield Garage
2001	November - John Seed retires
2001	December - huts demolished
2002	Jan - ICL remaining at Kidsgrove announce move to Crewe and end of ICL brand name by 2003
2002	Jan - Alstom announces up to 20 job cuts at Kidsgrove and move of Power Conversion sector into T & D sector
2002	Death of Lord Weinstock, Chairman of GEC
2004	April – 1st wind turbine (2.3MW) cubicle shipped to Bonus in Denmark
2004	June – 25 Years Anniversary of GEM80, re-union held
2004	June – visit to Kidsgrove by John Nixon, former Director and General Manager under GEC
2005	August – Demolition of ICL / Celestica works
2006	January – building work commences for giant distribution centre on old ICL site
2006	May 14th – Ian Gilmore, Gen. Manager, killed in motorbike accident on A34 at Siddington
2007	October – Plaque unveiled showing 2.5GW of energy shipped of wind turbine drives
2008	August – Demolition of Main GEC Works and Northfields
2012	Peak output of wind converters with up to 40 per week being supplied
2016	December – end of all production at Kidsgrove Southfields
2017	Kidsgrove site closes. Some staff relocated to Stafford, most made redundant.
2018	January – demolition work on Southfields office and factory commences

Appendix 2 Site Plan

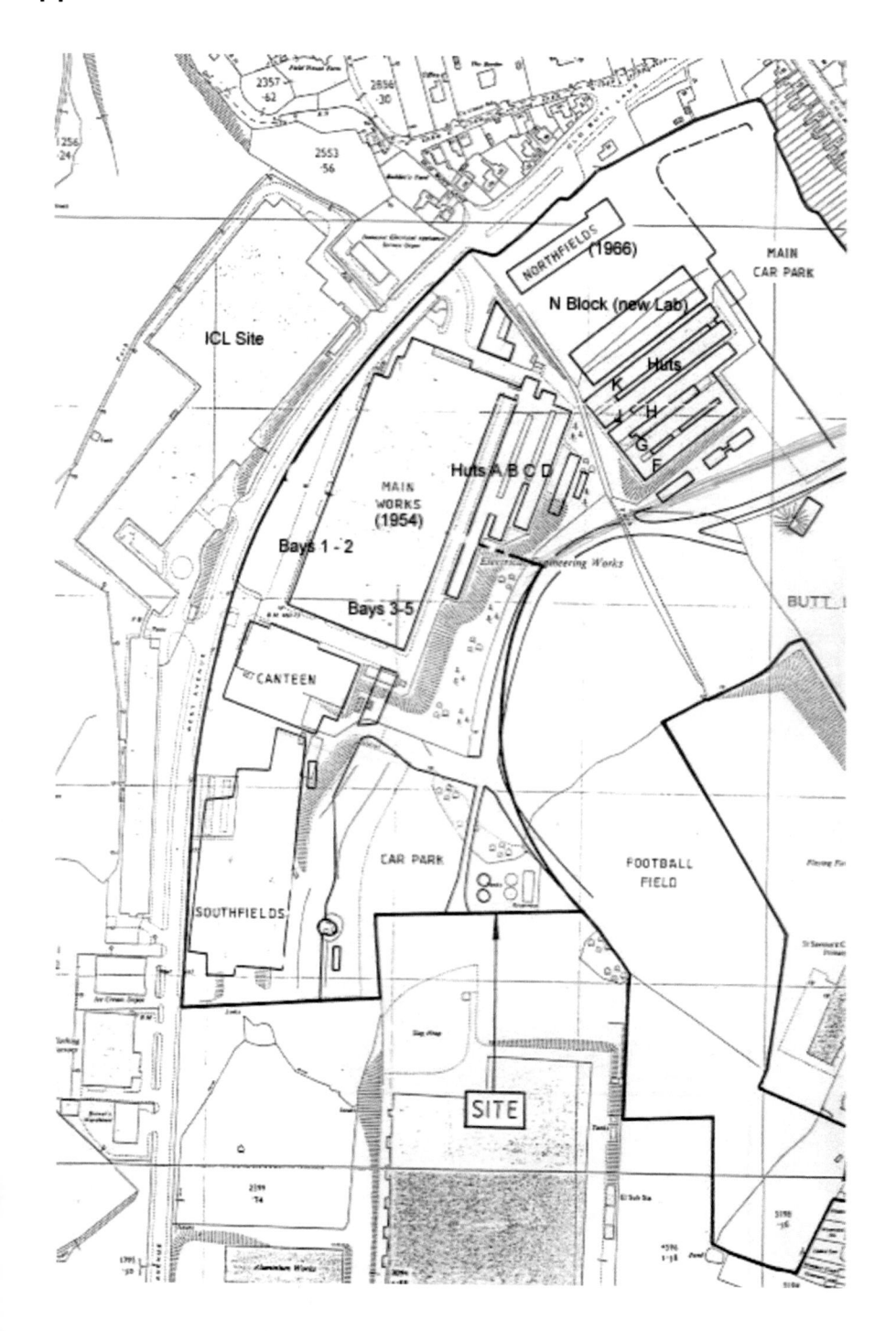

Appendix 3 – Company Logos/Letterheads

From 1953

ENGLISH ELECTRIC

From around 1969

GEC-Elliott Automation Ltd.
GEC-Elliott Industrial Controls Division
Kidsgrove Stoke-on-Trent Staffs ST7 1TW

Mid 1970s to 1989

GEC Industrial Controls Limited

1989 to 1999

CEGELEC

1999 to 2006

ALSTOM

2006 to 2011

CUSTOMIZING POWER CONVERSION SOLUTIONS

CONVERTEAM

93

Appendix 4 – AC DRIVES DEVELOPMENT AT KIDSGROVE

As we have seen, many new and innovative products were designed and developed at Kidsgrove. In fact, too many to detail in this book. However, one development was of such significance that it led to the site's single biggest product line in terms of both volume and sales. That product line was Wind Turbine Converters and the enabling development was that of AC Drives and the liquid cooled DELTA power module.

To give an idea of magnitude, back in the mid 1980's the GEM80 range of programmable controllers reached peak annual sales of £32M (at today's value). Nearly 30 years later, the wind converter sales reached a peak of £100M! Without the work done on AC drives technology, the successes in the renewables market would not have been possible and the site would have closed in about 2004.

Beginnings

From its beginning in 1954, Kidsgrove was renowned for the design and production of drives for DC motors which powered industries such as iron and steel, paper milling and mining. This situation remained until the 1980s by which time AC motors had gained widescale popularity due to the absence of brushes making contact with a commutator which wore out and required frequent maintenance. In the late 1950s, the semiconductor device known as the Thyristor (or SCR) made DC motor control fairly easy. The thyristor only allows current flow in one direction which is great for DC motors. The other feature is that when the AC mains cycle passes through zero, the thyristor automatically turns off. So the way you control a DC motor with a thyristor is to delay the moment in the mains cycle when the thyristor turns on. Turn it on at the start of the mains cycle then you get full power. Delay it and you can control the power down to zero. Furthermore, this delay is turning on requires only a resistor and a capacitor.

However, the thyristor is most unsuitable for the control of an AC motor where the current alternates at 50 or 60 cycles per second. This did not stop GEC engineers from trying which resulted in the development of a product called PHASAR at the start of the 1980s. The PHASAR drive used a thyristor bridge to convert the incoming mains to DC and then used thyristors to control the motor. A large capacitor bank was used to generate the reverse charge needed to turn the thyristor's off. The output was "Quasi-Square" and was very electrically noisy, but variable speed was possible. The PHASAR was not very reliable and did not last long.

Enter High Power - High Voltage Transistors

One step along the way to the development of the Kidsgrove AC drives was the use of newly available power transistors that were first used in DC drives for machine tool applications.

This resulted in the GEMDRIVE AXIS Mark 1 product and later the MKII versions (right). Both products were designed to drive permanent magnet DC motors with conventional commutators and brushes. The main developer behind the axis drive product, including the identification of the market requirements and market opportunities was Roger Critchley aided and abetted by Rod Jones who would go on to provide a key role in AC drives and wind turbine converter some ten years later.

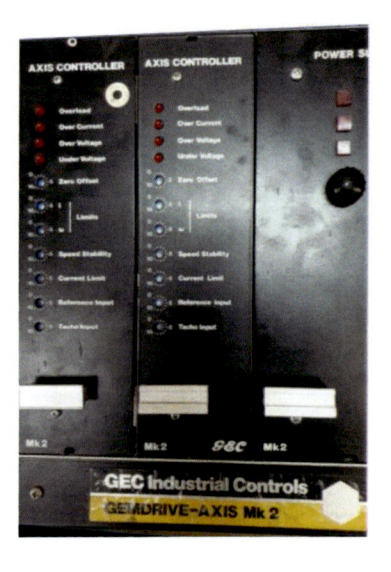

The axis drives incorporated bipolar transistors mainly from Thomson CSF. Thomson CSF were a French based semi-conductor company with a very capable applications engineering department that provided strong guidance in the use of their products, recommendations for base driver circuits, circuit layout to minimise inductance and so on. To drive a brushed dc motor, the basic circuit of the axis drive was a voltage sourced 'H-Bridge' comprising 4 'switches', 2 in each of 2 legs. Each 'switch' comprised a bipolar Darlington transistor made up of a first stage transistor driving into the base of multi-paralleled transistors to handle the total load current. Darlington configurations were widely used at that time to achieve high current ratings with relatively modest base drivers. Darlington configurations allowed the current gain of the two transistor stages forming the Darlington to be multiplied together. As the current gain of power transistors at that time may only be in the order of 10 or so, the Darlington configuration allowed current gain in the order of 100 to easily be achieved.

The voltage rating of the bipolar transistors used in axis drives would be in the 300 – 450 volt range. Consequently, to allow for transient switching over-shoot voltages, supply voltage transients, braking periods, etc., nominal dc link voltages of up to 250V were permissible. Such low voltage dc links would typically be derived from step-down transformers from the normal industrial supply voltage and 6 pulse rectification to create the dc link.

GEMDRIVE AXIS sold in high volumes to various machine tool manufacturers and it was from this baseline that 3-phase ac transistor drive development would begin.

Above: The lab of GEC Kidsgrove circa. 1976 where work on bipolar transistors for DC machine tool drives would pave the way for AC Drives later on. Engineers Ian Aitchison and John Gare

GEMDRIVE Spindle AC

Before we leave machine tool drives, we need to mention the GEMDRIVE Spindle AC. This product was a bipolar transistor based 'vector' controller, aimed primarily at the machine tool main spindle drive market for lathes, milling machines and machining centres.

The first prototype version used an 8 bit processor based on NEC7810 microprocessor, Jeremy Hinton was a key developer of this product under the leadership of Roger Critchley. The 7810 had a very similar instruction set to the Intel 8080. It was an interesting chip in its time as it had two sets of local registers that could be switched with a single instruction, this allowed the computation of the current references and slip angle in a program execution period which was (just) shorter than the pulse width modulation period of 1/4 kHz, or 250 µs.

1987 NIGEL GREATOREX AWARD

Rod Jones, a Principal Engineer working in the Drives Development Department at Kidsgrove, has been awarded a 'runners-up' prize in the 1987 Nigel Greatorex Award for his work on the development of GEMDRIVE-SPINDLE AC. This is a high performance Induction Motor Controller for Machine Tool Applications and his work had many varied aspects from high voltage transistors, switching at high frequency, to microprocessor based circuits for the complex control system and all the associated software.

The production versions of the Spindle drive adopted a 16 bit controller based on Intel 80186. This was also in essence a function generator now producing voltage and current references for analog current controllers and triangle wave type analog pulse width modulator. Again the switching frequency was 4 kHz, so the program execution period had to be less than 250 µs, otherwise the world would end!

The Spindle Drive used bipolar transistors with a thick film hybrid base driver that was process engineered and constructed by Steve Beattie, Gary Jones and the hybrid team in house. The hybrid was perhaps the most complicated that had been produced at Kidsgrove. Various tricks were incorporated; for example, to isolate different resistors in the overall circuit, diagonal cuts were made into the metalised lands to which circuit components such as IC's and capacitors would later be soldered. The individual resistors could then be trimmed to the design value without other resistors in the overall circuit network compromising the measurement. The circuit then was 'assembled' with the final soldering operation.

The first version of the hybrid base driver design suffered significant EMC (electro-magnetic compatibility) issues. These were overcome with the second version, which incorporated extra decoupling to the input stages, power supply rails, etc. The base drivers were mounted to a power board that then made direct mechanical connection to the 3 x dual bipolar transistor modules. The power board incorporated base drive power supplies and Hall effect current transducers.

The same base driver and associated power board were used in both GEMDRIVE SPINDLE AC and GEMDRIVE AXIS AC products.

The first production versions used a power supply module comprising a 6 pulse diode rectifier with a resistive dynamic brake facility, also known as a brake chopper.

The market trend was towards line regenerative power supplies, so that braking energy was returned to the supply network, rather than dissipating it as heat.

A line regenerative input module based on the known technology of thyristor bridges, combined with a 'H' bridge already known from the DC axis drives was designed. Circuit-wise, the DC terminals of a three-phase thyristor bridge are connected between the two 'phase' terminals of the H bridge, and the dc link feeds into the combination of axis and spindle drives connected to the input module. Power flow is then possible in both directions. There were many problems to overcome with this arrangement, not least the massive changes in operating point required for the H bridge pulse width modulator as the thyristor bridge provided a differing voltage depending on the instantaneous value of the incoming ac supply waveform. Feed-forward features were included into the current controller for the H bridge, which was known amongst the development group as the 'grand-canyon detector' as the operating point of the H bridge had to be changed significantly as the thyristors stepped from one firing group to the next every 3.3 ms. The product was not very successful, at it had all the issues of thyristor technology with network side harmonics and poor dynamic response.

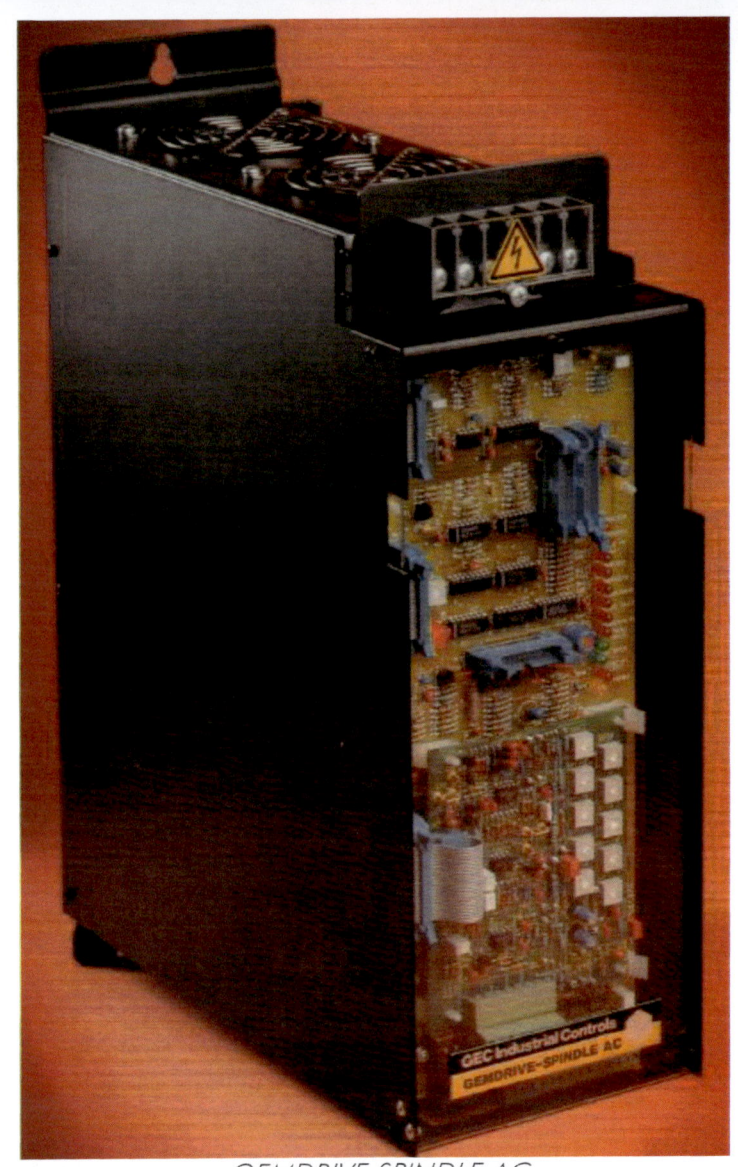

GEMDRIVE SPINDLE AC
GEC 1985

The PULSAR (1984)

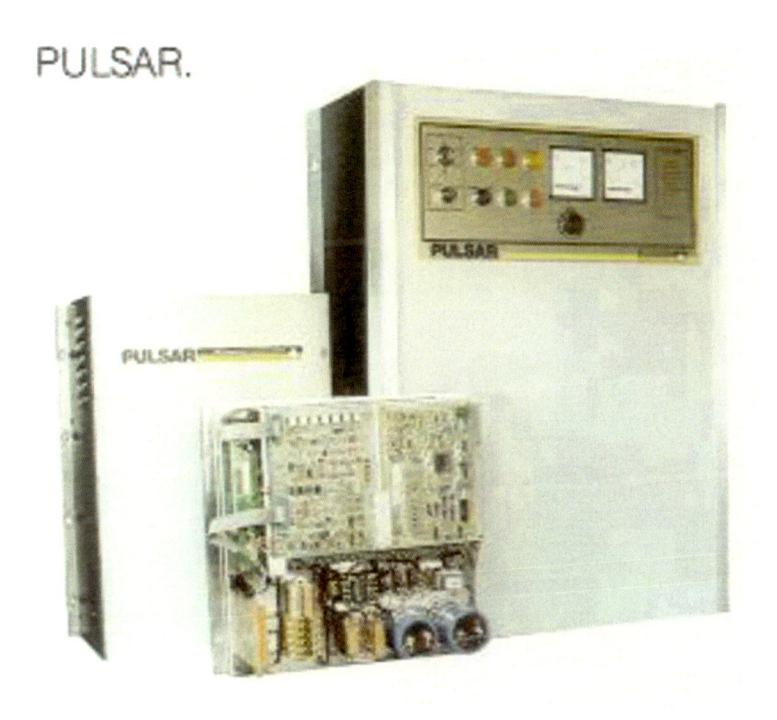

PULSAR.

The first fully transistorised drive for general purpose AC induction motors was the PULSAR. It featured a diode bridge input, providing a DC link and then bipolar transistor technology for power output switching. PULSAR was also microprocessor controlled, using the "Micro - Regulator". The PULSAR provided a pulse width modulated waveform (PWM) giving 300 - 600Hz output which provided a much better output waveform than the PHASAR drives. This drive came from the team at Rugby (GEC Industrial Controls, Mill Road) who had developed the Micro-Regulator originally for use in the first digital DC drive called GEMDRIVE MICRO 1 product, or GDM1 as it became known. It used an 80186 processor to achieve the control functions necessary for phase control, current control, and outer loop controls. To achieve high flexibility in system applications, it incorporated a cut-down GEM80 PLC running ladder program. This same Micro-Regulator provided the control for several AC drives thereafter. The power range was from 0.75kW to 55kW.

Pulse Width Modulation (PWM)

Before going further we should discuss the technique known as PWM - Pulse Width Modulation. This is the method employed by all the AC drives covered from Pulsar to MV3000. In PWM, the output is made up of a series of "blocks" or pulses of differing widths (or lengths of time). The transistor that switches on these pulses is either fully ON or fully OFF. The length of the ON time compared to the OFF time determines the output voltage.

The diagram below, from an old GEC publication, shows how the pulses start off small, then get wider and then smaller again. If this waveform is filtered and applied to a motor, the motor behaves as though it were seeing a sinewave voltage for practical purposes. When digital or microprocessor electronics are used to generate the PWM, then almost full control of a motor can be achieved by producing an output frequency from almost zero to say 300 or 600Hz. The actual switching frequency varies based on design and can range from 1.25kHz to 5 kHz or more.

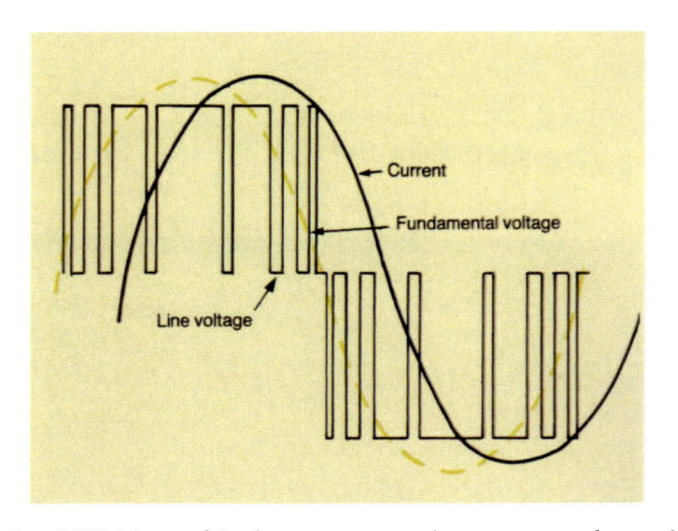

One reason that PWM is used is that power transistors operate best when they are either on or off – never half way. The formula for power is Voltage x Current. When the transistor is off the current – and hence power dissipated is zero. When the transistor is fully on, the current passed is multiplied by the voltage across the transistor which is typically 0.3V. So assuming a current of say 10A, the power is 10A x 0.3V = 3 Watts. Now assume the transistor is half on with say 10V across it. The power is then 10A x 10 V = 100 Watts. Therefore, having a switching transistor is more efficient than one that is providing linear control (such as in an audio amplifier for example).

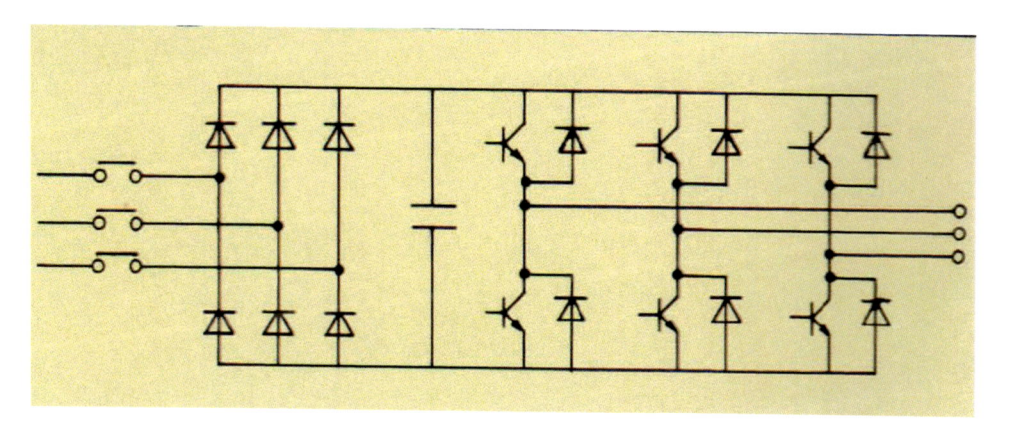

The diagram above shows the arrangement of the input diode bridge and output transistors on the Pulsar. However, this same topology would be common to all AC drives.

SL Drives and VF Drives - 1987

The next generation of AC drives were the SL and VF ranges from around 1987. They worked on a similar principle to the PULSAR but at an increased power range. They were cheaper and much more reliable. The higher power units used Gate Turn Off Thyristors or GTOs.

GEMDRIVE TB (1987) & SABRE (1990) DRIVES

Towards the end of the 1980s a new transistor type started to become available known as the insulated-gate bipolar transistor or IGBT. These devices were incorporated in the TB and SABRE drive ranges which had a switching frequency of some 6.6 kHz which provided a better output waveform.

The development for this was led by Ian Shaw. He set the target to achieve the first frame size at 7.5 kW with a footprint equivalent to an A4 page. At the time that Ian started the development, Toshiba introduced a viable 50A IGBT module. The gate drivers were self-powered and relied on the operation the inverter bridge to charge up the gate driver power supply capacitors

The Move to Big AC Drives with the GD2000/GD4000 Ranges

By 1992 all the elements were now in place at Kidsgrove for the site to move into much higher power AC drives. Furthermore, the name GEC had gone and Kidsgrove was now part of Cegelec – a French based firm. Lessons had been learned on the early AC drives covered previously and the firm had built up expertise with high power transistors and IGBTs initially with DC machine tool drives and then with the AC Spindle. The Kidsgrove team had a significant boost in 1987 when some of the AC drives development team from GEC Rugby joined the drives development group in Kidsgrove, all under the management of Roger Critchley. Mike Fulcher, Philip Waite and Tom Gowans moved up from Rugby, bringing with them their GEMDRIVE SL range and other advanced drive technology.

Development Manager Roger Critchley obtained development funding for a new range of fully digital AC drives. This was to be split into two distinctive developments:

- GD2000 – a 2 quadrant AC Product Drive Range – up to 500kW
- GD4000 – a 4 quadrant AC System Drive Range – up to 500kW

The two ranges should share as much in common as possible including the power stack, moldings and keypad.

> Terminology Note: Two Quadrant (2Q) operation means the drive provides forward and reverse motor control and takes power from the mains via a rectifier bridge. Four Quadrant (4Q) also provides forward and reverse motoring but now allows forward and reverse braking or regenerative power flow to and from the mains supply.

Two Controllers

To meet the needs of both the "simple" product drive and the system drive it was always clear that two different controllers would be required. For the GD4000 this would be the SIGMA controller and for the GD2000 range it would be the OMEGA controller.

GD2000 & The Omega Controller

Young engineers Rob Fulcher and Gary Pace had been working on reliability improvements to the TB and Sabre drives when they were put on a team to work in the GD2000 range. This featured a compact design with integral display and keypad on the front. The smallest drive was the GD2005 and the largest the GD2207 i.e. from 5A to 207A.

The Omega control board used the very new Siemens 80C166 microcontroller (20MHz), developed for engine management, (and soon used by McLaren in the F1 cars, and in the McLaren F1 roadcar). The first examples had a few hardware bugs in them, and Gary and Rob found a few of these, and helped Siemens (later Infineon) find, fix and test some of these bug fixes.
GD2000 was the open-loop, VVVF drive, with a few add-ons.

GD3000 & GD3000E

Then, a few years later, the team developed an encoder feedback board, and produced a vector control version of the GD2000, essentially sitting between GD2000 and GD4000, and hence called GD3000.

This took the control structure from GD4000 of 2 independent current control loops in D and Q and applied it to the GD2000 hardware. A new controller design was carried out for this incorporating the 167 processor in place of the 166 processor used in the GD2000. The new product allowed selection of VVVF or Vector in the same product by appropriate parameterisation.

GD3000 OMEGA Controller

Finally, around 1997, a new, more powerful control board using the C167 micro was developed, called Omega 2, (25MHz) for the GD3000E. This had VVVF, vector control, and later encoderless vector control.

The GD4000 SIGMA Controller

The SIGMA controller originated from the large drives development team in Rugby and would be adapted for the new GD4000. It comprised an INTEL 960CA 32-bit RISC based processor and XILINX field programmable gate array (FPGA) as the counter/timer block to create the actual PWM edge events.

The communications between 960 and XILINX were the subject of significant discussions between Kidsgrove and Rugby engineers. The objective was to have a common interface that would then allow all classes of large drive – DC, SyncDrive, IMDrive, Cycloconverters, etc. – and GD4000 all to be controlled with their respective switch count and PWM period or fast task rate. The range of control requirements that had to be accommodated was massive.

The eventual solution can be visualised as an etch-a-sketch combined with a Gattling gun. Two arrays of registers were set-up in the XILINX, each register was sufficient to contain the entire control word necessary to give the signals to the sub-ordinate device drivers. The number of registers in each array was determined by the required edge timing resolution of final control signal and the number of PWM quanta in a given fast task period. So for example, in GD4000 the switching frequency was 3.3 kHz so the fast task period was 300 µs, and the edge timing resolution was 330 ns. Two arrays of registers were included to page between on a per fast task basis.

During a given fast task period, one array would be providing the switching events, whilst the other array would be written to by the 960 at the end of its calculation of new switching events and states.

All registers would be set to NO CHANGE on initialisation. The 960 would then write PWM status commands to the relevant registers in say register array 1, where the register address related to the point in the PWM period when the command was to be issued. So for GD4000 with 2 x 6 pulse bridges, a total of 24 registers would have to be written to by the 960. At the start of the next fast task period when array 1 was to be active to issue output states to the power devices, then the registers in array 1 would be scrolled through. As most registers would be filled with NO CHANGE data, then only those registers with state change data would result in a change. Some mechanism was included to rub-out already executed state changes so that the register was set back to a NO CHANGE state ready for the next but one fast task.

Senior Drives Development Engineer Rod Jones with the Rt. Hon. Michael Heseltine MP – the GD4000 had just won the 1992 TRIAD Award for product of the year

There was some controversy from some in the Kidsgrove engineering team at the time in joining forces for the SIGMA development with Rugby. Some of this controversy related to the age old problem of 60,000 versus 40,000 series software. Rugby had created a higher performance set of software modules and special functions, known as 60,000 series modules, but restricted their use to the Rugby systems and so prevent Kidsgrove making direct sales of product drives such as GDM1 and GD4000 to would be system integrators that could perhaps undercut Rugby to the final customer.

A well-worn statement from engineer Mike Frenda was that 'more people could fly the space shuttle than could program a GD4000'. It was a complicated system to work with, fast task modules had to be joined together to form a particular drive control requirement within a fast task written and compiled by development engineers. Connections from slow task to fast task were organised by a links program, which could be written by applications engineers using the toolbox provided. A further level of programming existed at the ladder level where conventional GEM80 PLC ladder code was included to give a high degree of application level flexibility to the product.

At this time there was a lot of competition in the control systems industry to find a communication protocol between PLC's, Drives and other control elements in a complete plant. SIGMA was developed to support up to 4 additional plug in expansion cards, and communication cards were produced for various existing and emerging communication protocols.

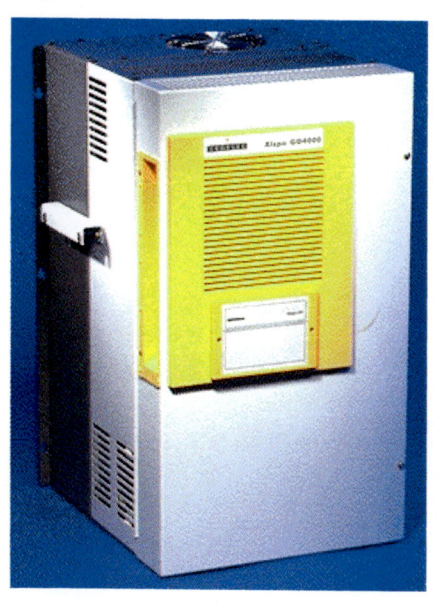

GD4000 BDM with front mounted SIGMA Controller

GD2207/GD4160 and the Birth of the DELTA Module

The largest basic drive modules (BDM's) in the GD2000/GD4000 range were GD2207 and GD4160 respectively with the last three digits meaning amps. These used 3 x 400A dual IGBT modules from Fuji Electric in the GD2207 and 6 of the same IGBT module in the GD4160.

Cegelec was an international organization with each unit tending to compete for central development funds and prestige. The development group in Macon USA produced a prototype phase module intended for operation in single or multi-paralleled arrangement. This was an air-cooled arrangement with an accordion type bellows arrangement connecting to the top of the assembly to connect to the cubicle mounted ventilation system. Various engineers in Kidsgrove drives development saw this arrangement as a threat to our future if it were to be sanctioned for full development into a product. In the evening immediately following a key HQ meeting, the existing GD4160 CAD design was rearranged to remove the SIGMA controller, power supply, I/O board and fan. The resulting 6 phase bridge was then re-connected as a 3 phase bridge with 800A of silicon in each switch, so forming what was later to be known as a GDD377-4401 (GDD=Gemdrive Delta). The assembly was then turned through 90 degrees in the CAD system to form a bookcase style module rated at 377A. The beauty of this was that several modules could be connected in parallel.

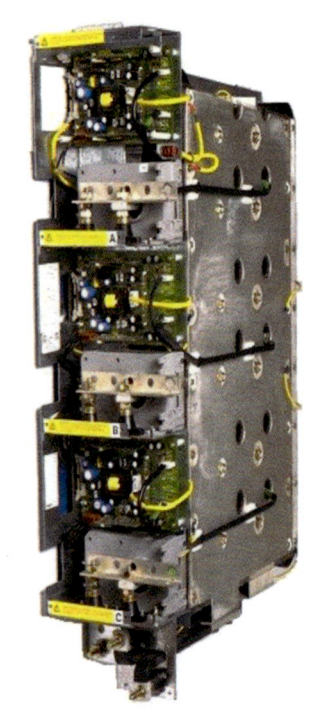

GDD377 DELTA Mk1 MODULE

Initially they were arranged into 3 parallel and 6 parallel groups to form ratings of GD21131 and GD41131 respectively. Fans were added above, with a sloping interface avoiding the need for the bellows of the Macon design. An underslung air-cooled reactor assembly provided the inter-bridge sharing inductance. The resulting assembly was then presented the next day as the DELTA system. DELTA modules were further developed into full products and provided the basis of the Cegelec high current rating ac product drives for many years.

In spite of efforts to use IGBT modules graded for the forward voltage drop of the free-wheel diodes, the natural current sharing of the GDD377 in parallel configurations was not very good. In early systems, additional output resistance had to be added in each DELTA phase by splitting the cable to the load into separate conductors.

To overcome the issue of current sharing between DELTA phases, Philip Waite, Rob Fulcher and Gary Pace designed an active sharing system based on the premise that if the current in a given DELTA phase was bigger than the average current in all like phases, then subtract a small time element of the IGBT ON signal to that phase. The active sharing system was implemented in both GD2000 and GD4000.

Enter SKiiP®2

The GDD377 was rated for up to 800V dc link operation using 1200V rated IGBTs. To address the emerging market for 690V fed drives, a solution using 1700V IGBT modules was required.

Around this time period, SEMIKRON (in Germany) were introducing their SKiiP® 2 product with versions available at 1200V and 1700V. The SKiiP® 2 product opened up the possibility of a DELTA product with both 900V and 1200V dc link ratings, so answering all Kidsgrove large ac drive requirements with two build versions of what was to be a Mark II Air Cooled DELTA product in 1997. So, based on SKiiP®2, GDD377-4501 and GDD300-4601 were developed. Furthermore, by using the GD3000E controller, it was possible to connect six modules in parallel giving ratings of 2262A for the 380/415V

DELTA MkII SKiiP®2 Based

operation and 1800A for 600/690V AC operation using the 300A Deltas. A range of air-cooled rectifiers had been developed to provide the input to the Delta system. These rectifiers were designed to fit into the same cross rail mounting system and again, rectifiers could be paralleled up to achieve the higher ratings. Early SKiiP® 2 was not the most reliable of products at the time and many months were spent investigating failures and incorporating remedies.

How the DELTA Module Operates

The diagram below is representative of any DELTA module. Three SKiiP® power modules form the heart of it. When used to control an AC motor, DC power is applied to the DC terminals from a suitably rated rectifier module. This input power charges up a very large bank of capacitors to create what is called the DC Link. This can be from around 700V to over 1000V depending on mains supply etc.

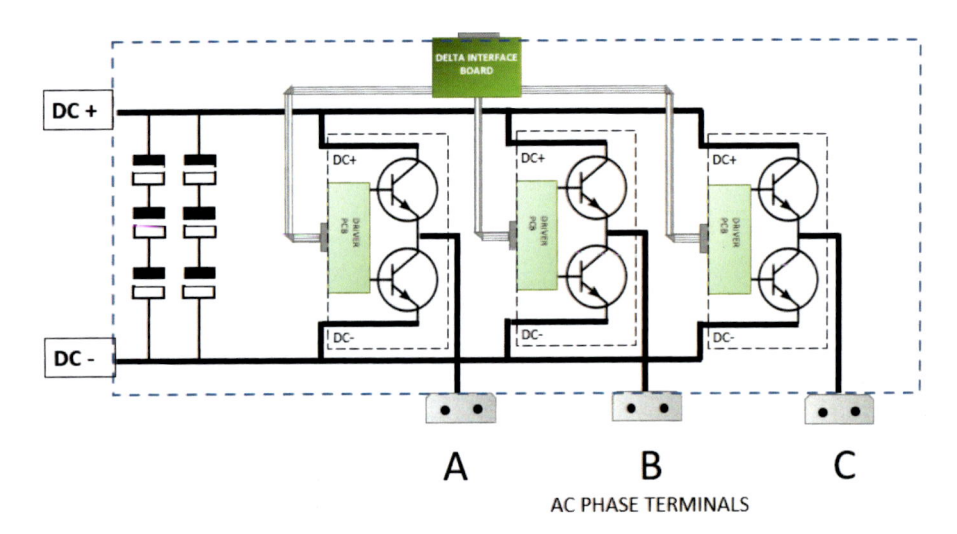

A   B   C
AC PHASE TERMINALS

Switching signals from the controller are routed via the Delta Interface Board (DIB) and then passed to each SKiiP®. These signals are Pulse Width Modulated (PWM) where the period of on to off time is adjusted very rapidly to give the required AC output voltage. As there are three branches then an approximation to a three phase AC signal is produced at the output. The output waveform is far from the clean sinewave of the original mains but due to the inductance and inertia of the motor, this is not really a problem and in practice excellent motor control can be achieved. We must also mention at this point that there is a lot going on inside the SKiiP®'s driver board. It is providing current and temperature feedback as well as protection against mis-firing. These signals travel via the DIB back to the CDC controller.

The First Liquid Cooled DELTA 1MW Wind Turbine

There was interest, particularly encouraged by Jack Noakes of Renewable Energy Systems (RES), to increase the power density of the air-cooled DELTA product by making a water cooled product.

With encouragement from Jack, and much form filling, a 50% contribution, amounting to something like £200,000, was obtained from a UK Government agency known as the Energy Technology Support Unit (ETSU) towards the development cost of a liquid cooled DELTA module targeting the renewable energy sector, and in particular wind turbines.

The first version used an available liquid cooled heatplate from Semikron to which was attached a 4-bay SKiiP® 2 rated at 1000A 1700V. This allowed a target rating of 643 amps rms to be proposed, allowing for a 1.1 overload above the continuous rating. Two castings connected three of the liquid cooled heatplates in hydraulic parallel.

A prototype was built and run successfully in laboratory trials.

By putting the three heatsinks in hydraulic parallel, the issue of stack rise was eliminated, however because the coolant was distributed between three heatsinks, the flow velocity through each heatsink was low and heat transfer was not as effective.

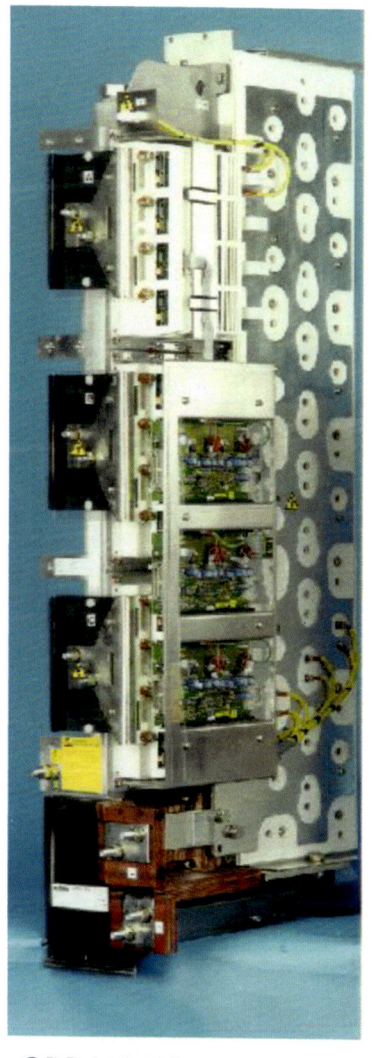

GDD643 LIQUID COOLED DELTA

A design was then created for a liquid cooled inverter assembly with 3 heatplates arranged in hydraulic series, with a single casting providing the chassis in which the three heatplates were mounted. The resulting product was known as GDD643-4601 and had a rating of about 600 kW on a 690V ac supply. It stood about 1.2m tall.

One of the first applications for this product was the 1 MW Renewable Energy Systems (RES) turbine that was erected in Antrim, Northern Ireland. This comprised 4 x GDD643-4601 as 2 network and 2 generator bridges connected to a GD4000 controller. Packaging of these inverters, programming the interface and initial commissioning was carried out by Mike Meakin and his group in Packaged Products in 1999.

Above: The 1MW RES Wind Turbine was the first to use the Liquid Cooled Delta

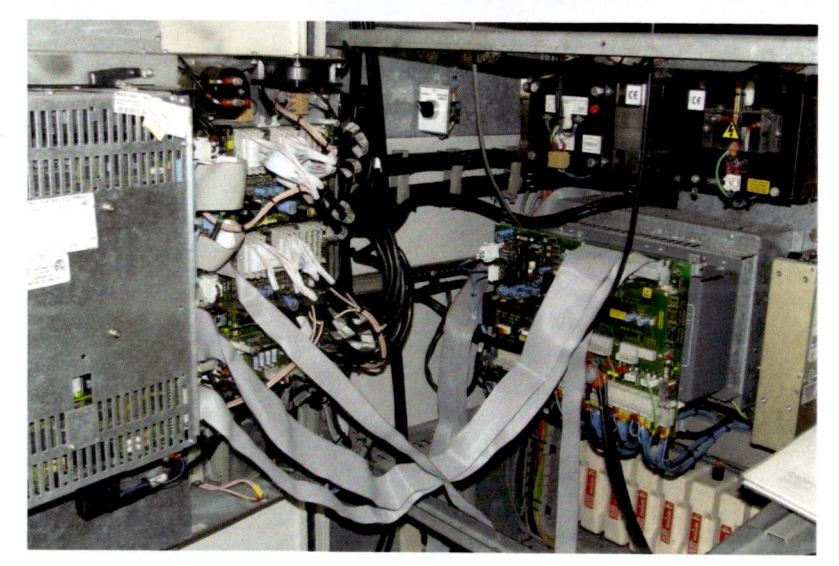

Above: Part of the RES converter. The SIGMA controller is on the left which is connected to interface circuits and power supplies on the right. It is amazing that this ever worked!

5th October 1998 - A landmark moment, the production of the first liquid cooled DELTA AC power module (GDD643-4701) pictured here are John Poole, Steve Beattie, Jeff Corbin, Rod Jones, Andy Chilton, Mick Daniels, Hadrian Smith, Martin Leake and Dave Mayer. This unit was shipped to customer Lonne A/S in Norway

SKiiP®3

SKiiP®2 incorporated IGBT chips from Infineon with freewheel diodes from Semikron. Improvements in IGBT technology by way of reducing saturated on-state voltage and reducing switching losses allowed increased current ratings to be achieved in the same chip area. This then allowed the module ratings to increase significantly. To handle the increased current rating, higher current rating current sensors, busbar connections, etc, a new SKiiP® was introduced. This was and is still known as SKiiP®3.

SKiiP®3 allowed the current rating of the GDD643 to be increased to 800A and later, through further increases in ac terminal cross sections, dc laminate cross sections and dc link capacitor sizes in the DELTA assembly, to 1000A.

MV3000 – New Range of AC Drives for the new Millennium

In 1996 Cegelec acquired the drives business of AEG in Berlin. The factory was huge and they produced a vast range of drives from small BDMs right up to tens of megawatts at voltages of 3 and 6KV etc. There was now a conflict as to who should develop the new drive range for Cegelec – either Kidsgrove or Berlin. A compromise was reached and the development would be shared. Berlin's drive range was called MD2000 and Kidsgrove has the GD3000E. The new drive range would be called MV3000 with the MV standing for Multi Verter which was becoming a standard set of initials for drive products across Cegelec at the time.

The requirements specification for MV3000 was provided by the Product Marketing Department, and in particular Roger Critchley in his new role now having moved on from Product Development Manager.

A bookcase style product drive was called for with a fully integrated controller, I/O and the option for supply side rectifier and dynamic brake switch. Kidsgrove had already established a prototype for a bookcase style 75 kW drive in the form of MINI-DELTA. At one of the initial meetings for MV3000, Philip Waite and Tom Gowans amongst others lugged the prototype MINI-DELTA to Berlin in a suitcase including dragging it between terminals at a transfer in Dusseldorf. It has been said many times, that including 'believable bold' in a presentation or hand-out is a very simple way of winning an argument between rival development groups, it is even more effective when a fully operational 3D prototype of a inverter solution is brought out of a suitcase at a meeting in Berlin!

The MV3000 requirement specification was for a total range of 7 frame sizes, 1 – 7. In fact only 4 frame sizes were produced from frame size 3 at 37 kW to frame size 7 at 315 kW. Above that rating, air cooled and liquid cooled DELTA configurations were available with connectivity for up to 6 in parallel for any group of network or generator bridges. A new interface was needed on the DELTA modules, and so a small product redesign took place and part numbers became MVDxxx and MVDLxxx(x) for air cooled and liquid cooled respectively. This allowed drive sizes up to 6 MW to be configured as 4Q ac drives with a total of 12 x MVDL1000 inverters. The new controller was called the CDC which stands for Common Drive Controller and is shown below.

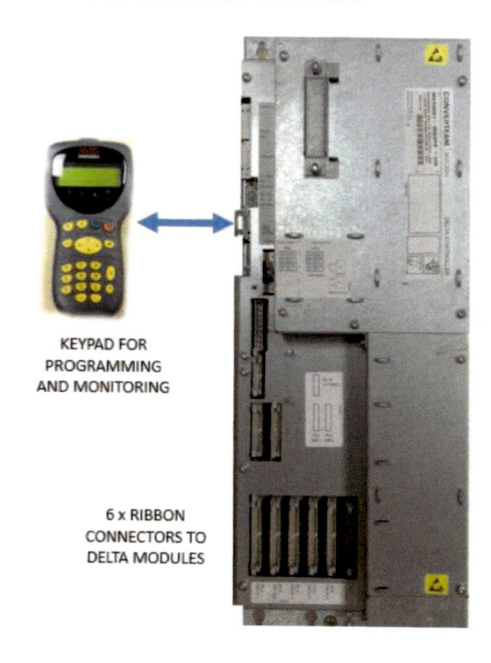

Frame Size 3 MV3000

KEYPAD FOR PROGRAMMING AND MONITORING

6 x RIBBON CONNECTORS TO DELTA MODULES

In the Berlin factory, their existing MD2000 range of drives was using Logicad - a very good programming language. Their controller was also based on the C167 processor same as the GD3000E. So originally the new controller was to use Logicad and was named the Common Drive Controller as it was to be used by all drives in all factories. However, the plan to use Logicad did not work and in order to get a drive to market in a timely manner, Gary Pace ported the software from GD3000E to MV3000 CDC. In practice, this worked out very well as the many man-years of GD development became available to the new MV3000 range and provided a fairly simple upgrade path for customers switching from the GD range to the new drives.

Price and Size Reductions for Small AC Drives

One of the key aims of technology development is the reduction in both cost and size of the product. This was true of AC drives and the chart below shows how a 75kW Drive unit occupied a volume of some 1.2m^3 in the early 1980s reducing to only 0.16m^3 in 1999. Over the same period, the cost reduced from £17k to £6k.

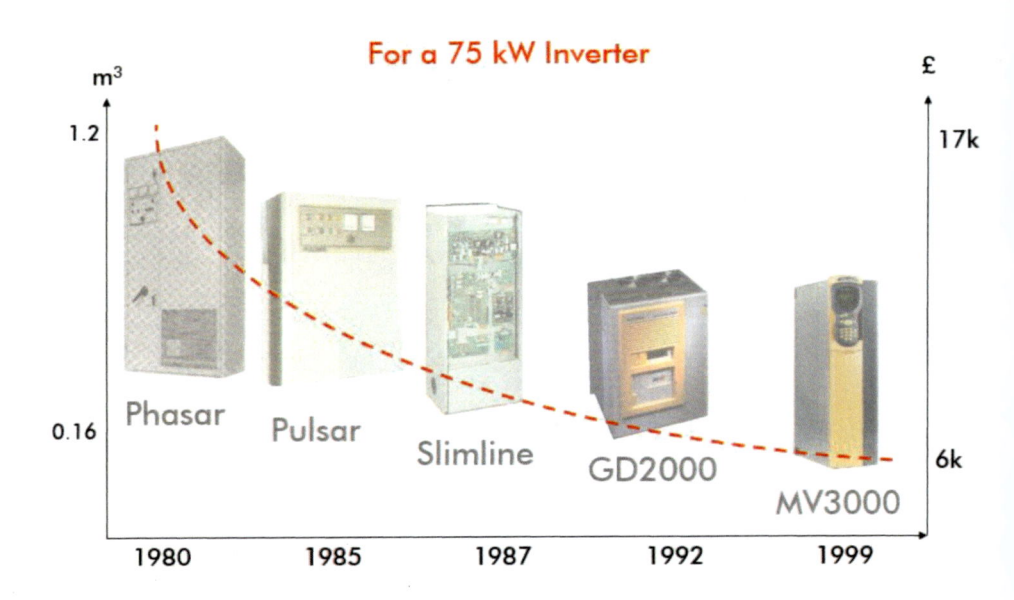

For a 75 kW Inverter

Year	Model	Volume (m³)	Cost (£)
1980	Phasar	1.2	17k
1985	Pulsar		
1987	Slimline		
1992	GD2000		
1999	MV3000	0.16	6k

The Start of the Large Scale Wind Turbine Business

As the GD4000 drive operated in all four quadrants, it could be used "in reverse" so to speak i.e. taking power from a generator and putting it back into the mains grid. As early as 1993, Sales Manager Ian Gilmore and Rod Jones made many visits to Denmark for discussions with the turbine designers and system solution providers to that developing market.

Key to these discussions was Henrik Stiesdal of Bonus Wind Energy. Stiesdal is regarded as the father of the modern wind turbine concept and built his first turbines in the 1970s. The first prototype GD4000 solution was deployed on a 90 kW turbine situated in

Ian Gilmore

the car park at the old Bonus Wind Energy factory in Brande, Denmark. There were many problems experienced at initial commissioning mainly due to the phasing of generator and shaft encoder. If the phasing was wrong, the inverter would operate at full current and full slip, but at zero speed. Operating in this mode for too long would lead to equipment damage.

Kidsgrove later provided a 600 kW solution, again based on GD4000 (**GD41131**) and air cooled GDD377 modules. This was system integrated by KK Electronics under the leadership of Peter Horsager from Bonus Energy. Dave Buckley of the customer support team in Kidsgrove was heavily involved in the initial commissioning. A period of co-operation was entered into between Bonus and Cegelec. This involved simulations, software and lab work at Kidsgrove plus field trials in Denmark.

Technical Note

Although induction generator wind turbines had been around for many years, virtually all these were based on a Doubly Fed Induction Generator (DFIG). In the DFIG design the converter only controls about 30% of the full power via separate windings. Converters to control the full power were not available in these early years. All the converters made at Kidsgrove were rated for the full power of the generator and allowed for a wider and more controlled operating range.

Melvin Heath wiring up a GD4000 high performance AC drive around 1994. This same equipment provided the prototype for the 600kW fully controlled wind turbine converter installed at Bonus Energy

To support Bonus, Kidsgrove made a major investment in 1995 in the form of a motor – generator set. These were 2 x 750kW AC "Flowpack" machines supplied from the firms Rugby factory. The machines were delivered in November ready for testing to commence early in 1996. This test rig was called "the Bonus Rig".

There were enormous technical difficulties to be overcome by both sides and progress was very slow due to issues with both the turbine and the converter design. As we saw earlier, the first Liquid Cooled Drive had been supplied to RES in Northern Ireland in 1999 using the GD643 Delta modules but the new requirement was for much bigger powers. By the end of 1999, Cegelec had developed its new MV3000 drive range.

It took two developments – the MV3000's CDC and the increased rating of the liquid cooled Delta to move things forward from the early air-cooled Sigma design. At the start of 2003, the first liquid cooled delta was supplied to Bonus as product converter. By the end of that year, the 800A delta replaced the 643A unit as the mainstay of the wind converter.

Ian Gilmore saw that if Kidsgrove supplied the whole converter cubicle, then this would be of maximum benefit to the company and would allow Bonus to concentrate on the rest of the turbine system.

A contract was drawn up and the first 2.3 MW cubicle was shipped in April of 2004, nearly 10 years after the first GD proto-type. When on December 1st 2004 the German electrical giant Siemens bought Bonus Energy A/S there were fears that the contract may be under threat. However, this was not the case and the new owners SWP (Siemens Wind Power) continued to buy Converteam equipment. In fact the business increased month on month. In 2007, after only 3 years of production, converter sales approached £50M.

In this Early Model 2.3MW Wind Converter the Deltas for the Network Bridge and Generator Bridge sit side by side

Basic 2.3MW Turbine Converter Operation

The induction generator is cabled back to the converter and is applied to a Generator Bridge comprising of 3 x 800A Delta modules. A CDC Generator controller switches this power into the DC Links of each Delta. These in turn are connected to a Network Bridge comprising of another 3 x 800A Delta modules which are under the control of a Network CDC.

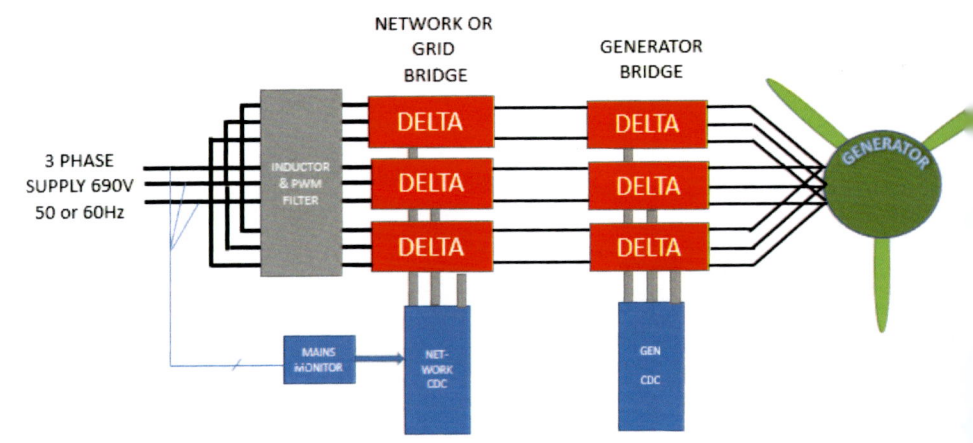

Both the input power from the generator and the output power to the network are both under the control of the MV3000 converter system. This means that for a wide range of wind speeds the converter can maintain a fixed voltage and fixed frequency output to the network. This is of course oversimplified and there are many other things going on which are not shown. One of which is the overall turbine control system which controls the pitch and yaw of the blades. It also looks after communication with both the converter and the outside world and provides protection systems.

Low Voltage Ride-Through (LVRT)

As the proportion of wind turbines that were connected to a given power network (grid) increased, so their characteristics had to change as they needed to share in the fault rating of the power network. In former times, in the event of low voltage events on the supply network, the converter was expected to trip out and disconnect from the power network and so prevent the back-feed of power into the network. The emerging requirement, which is still evolving to this day, was that turbines should remain connected and, depending on the specific grid code, provide active or reactive power or current up to the rating of the turbine. This feature was known as Grid Fault Ride-through or Low Voltage Ride-Through.

The initial investigations into this feature were carried out by an ex-Rugby SIGMA developer, Nick Elliott, working as sub-contractor to Kidsgrove, then the later stages of design and development were carried out mainly by Paul Brogan and Paul Godridge.

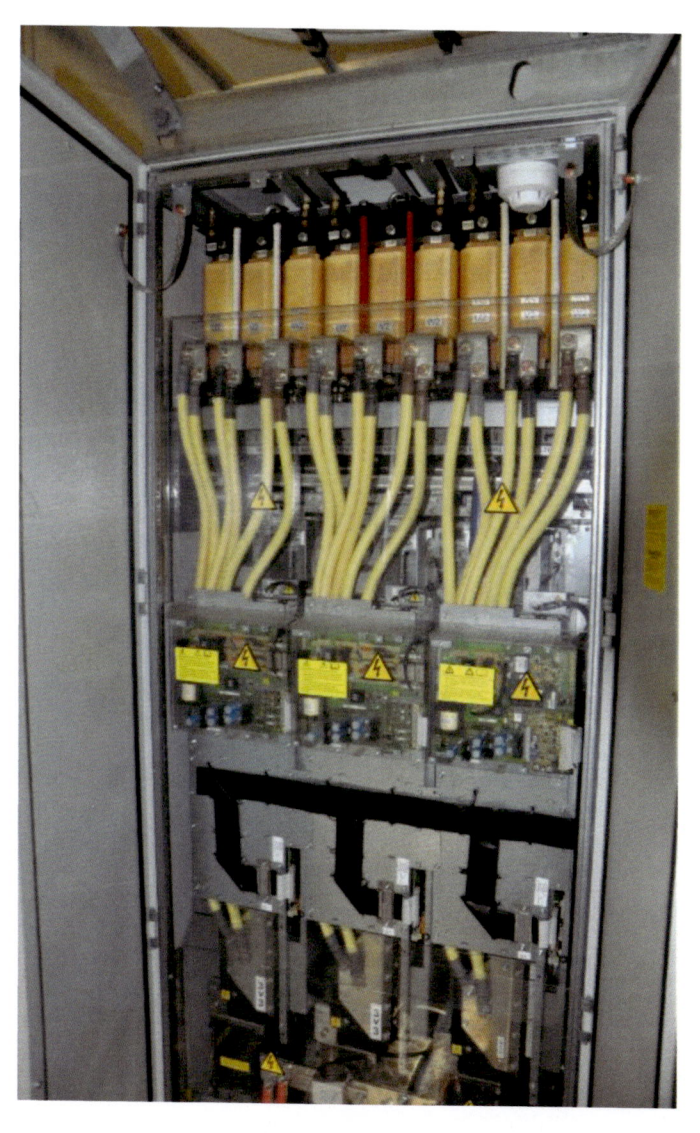

Above: An internal view of a later model 2.3 MW Wind Turbine Converter installed in a nacelle. In this type the network bridge and generator bridge Deltas are in a back to back arrangement. It was thought that this was the most compact of any converter in the world at 2.3MW

Evolution of the 2.3MW Wind Turbine Converter

The 2.3MW Wind Turbine Converter underwent many improvements over a ten year period. Many of these changes were brought about by cost reduction pressures as the marketplace demanded an ever decreasing product cost.

Production Line at Converteam Kidsgrove Factory 2007

Wind Converters were built on an assembly line and with this early set up shown above a maximum of 16 converters could be made each week. As demand ramped up, the whole line was radically overhauled allowing production to reach up to 40 converters per week a few years later. This was a remarkable achievement for a small factory and came about by the introduction of techniques used in the car industry (Hoshin/Kaizen).

The 3.6MW Wind Turbine Converter

Around 2009 a requirement arose for a high power design for use primarily in offshore wind farms. The generator power was to be 3.6MW.

In order to work at 3.6MW, four 1000A Delta modules were required for each bridge. This resulted in two converter cubicles, one in the tower base and one in the nacelle. The DC link cables connected the two parts as shown in the diagram below. A large number of these designs are in use off UK waters, the biggest site being London Array with some 175 turbines.

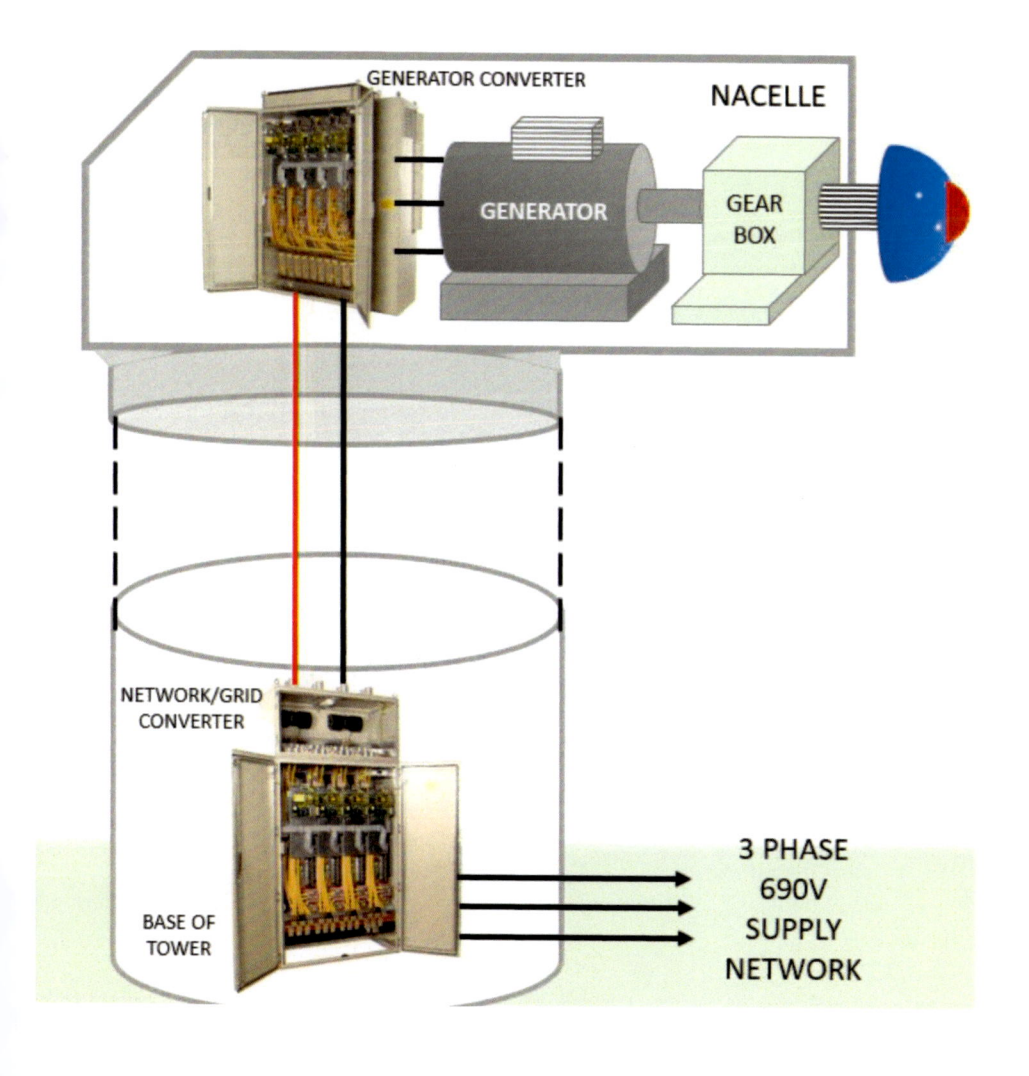

Conclusion

Pioneering work with high power/high voltage transistors in the 1980s enabled Kidsgrove to develop a range of AC PWM drives in the 1990s aided by expertise from a few members of the Rugby drives team. Two valuable cooperation projects with RES and Bonus Wind Energy allowed prototype wind converters to be developed. Many man-years of software development in the GD controllers was put to good effect in the MV3000 controller. The introduction of liquid cooling of the DELTA power module combined with the MV3000 CDC allowed Kidsgrove site to develop cost effective wind converters up to 3.6MW. Lean manufacturing methods enabled Kidsgrove to reach a peak output of some 40 converters per week.

Finally, it is widely recognized that site leader Ian Gilmore played a key role in turning his vision for the survival and growth of the business into reality.

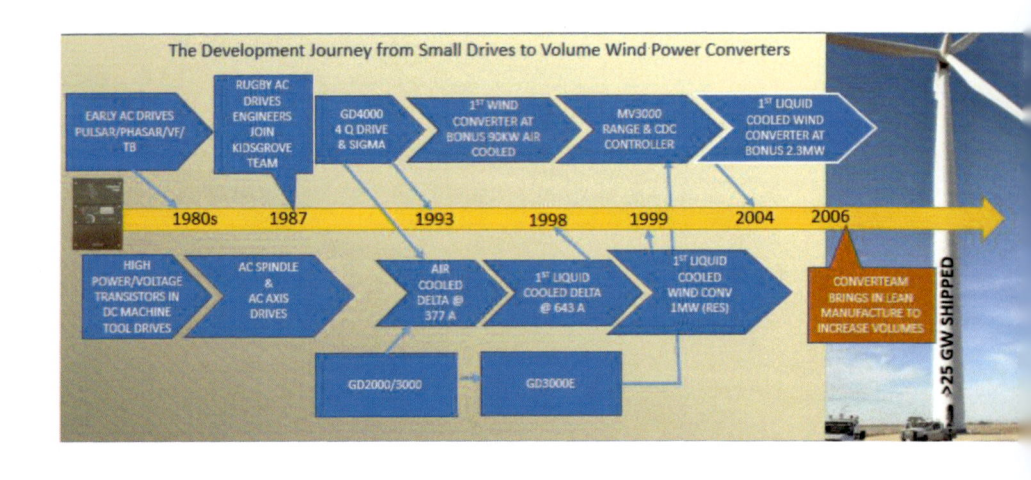

The Development Journey from Small Drives to Volume Wind Power Converters

Year	Above Timeline	Below Timeline
1980s	EARLY AC DRIVES PULSAR/PHASAR/VF/TB	HIGH POWER/VOLTAGE TRANSISTORS IN DC MACHINE TOOL DRIVES
1987	RUGBY AC DRIVES ENGINEERS JOIN KIDSGROVE TEAM	AC SPINDLE & AC AXIS DRIVES
1993	GD4000 4 Q DRIVE & SIGMA	AIR COOLED DELTA @ 377 A
1998	1ST WIND CONVERTER AT BONUS 90KW AIR COOLED	1ST LIQUID COOLED DELTA @ 643 A
1999	MV3000 RANGE & CDC CONTROLLER	1ST LIQUID COOLED WIND CONV 1MW (RES)
2004		GD2000/3000, GD3000E
2006	1ST LIQUID COOLED WIND CONVERTER AT BONUS 2.3MW	CONVERTEAM BRINGS IN LEAN MANUFACTURE TO INCREASE VOLUMES

>25 GW SHIPPED

Appendix 5 - A Brief History of ICL Kidsgrove

The giant ICL factory dominated the west side of the Nelson Industrial Estate and was thought of as the rich relation to the GEC side. Although I never worked at ICL and never had much archive material from there, I feel it is right to include a short summary of its history in this appendix. Many production operators joined the Converteam side of the site after the factory closed.

Beginnings

Computers have been made on the ICL site at Kidsgrove, Staffordshire from around 1962 when the factory was part of English Electric. During the mid 1960's there were two main computer manufacturers in Britain: ICT (International Computers and Tabulators Ltd) and English Electric Computers. There were a host of smaller players still around that had not already been swallowed up by the two main firms.

Each company had enjoyed success with the first generation computers but all now came under threat from the giant IBM and other USA companies with their advanced second-generation machines. At the time the Labour Government was in power and premier Harold Wilson realised that the British computer industry was in danger of collapse unless something was done to fight off the competition. Each of the separate UK firms were also using different standards in terms of computer architecture and media such as punched cards. Using the powers provided by the

Industrial Expansion Act a series of mergers were forced through to provide one large UK computer firm which culminated in the creation of ICL in 1968. ICL was essentially a forced merger between English Electric Leo Marconi Computers and ICT. In this part the history of ICL is covered.

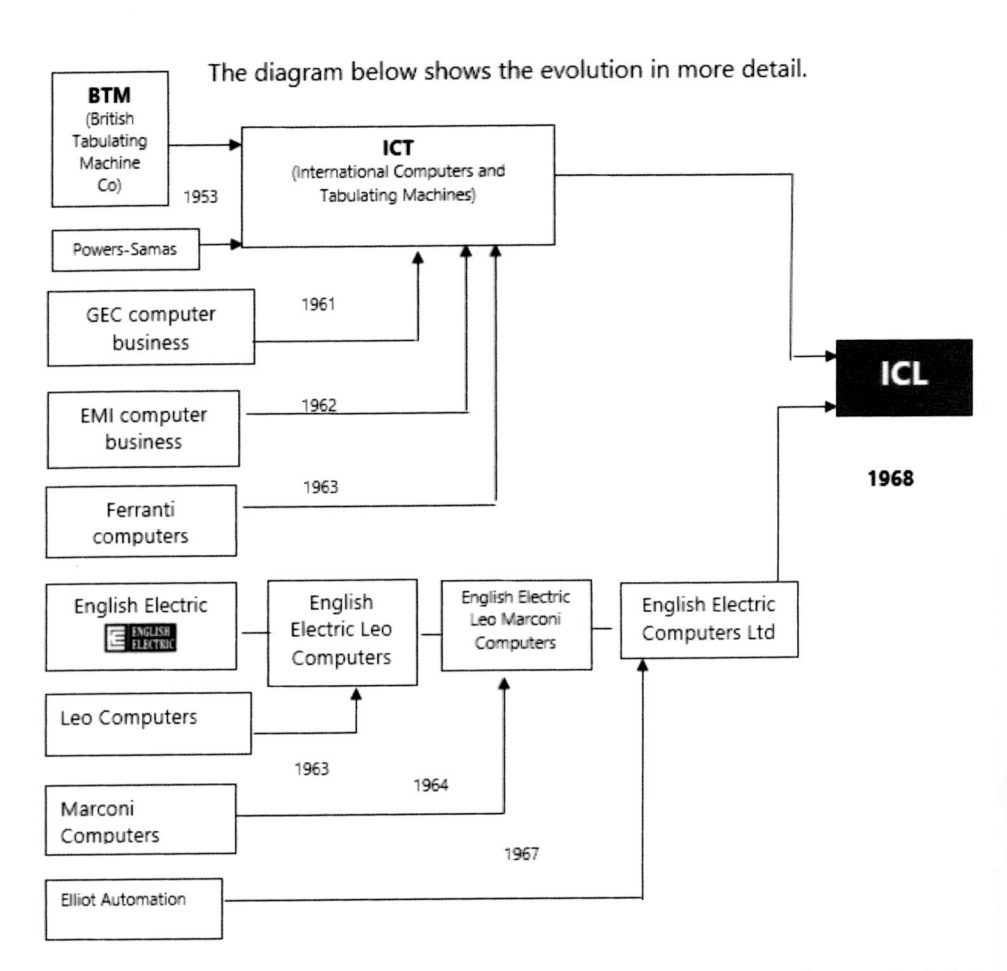

The diagram below shows the evolution in more detail.

```
BTM (British Tabulating Machine Co) ──1953──┐
                                            ├──► ICT (International Computers and Tabulating Machines) ──┐
Powers-Samas ───────────────────────────────┘                                                             │
                                                                                                          │
GEC computer business ──1961──────────────────►                                                           │
                                                                                                          ├──► ICL  1968
EMI computer business ──1962──────────────────►                                                           │
                                                                                                          │
Ferranti computers ──1963─────────────────────►                                                           │
                                                                                                          │
English Electric ──┐                                                                                      │
                   ├──► English Electric Leo Computers ──┐                                                │
Leo Computers ─────┘                                     ├──► English Electric Leo Marconi Computers ──┐  │
                           1963                          │                                              ├──► English Electric Computers Ltd ──┘
Marconi Computers ───────────────────────1964────────────┘                                              │
                                                                                                        │
Elliot Automation ──────────────────────────────────1967────────────────────────────────────────────────┘
```

Building started on the main ICL Kidsgrove works in July 1961 and was scheduled for completion by the summer of the following year. English Electric had purchased six acres of land from the council at a price of £2,000/acre. The main works was modelled on the Marconi Instruments works at St. Albans and cost around £311,000.

In 1967 more space was required and the firm Taylor Woodrow were commissioned to construct a new five-storey office block at the southern end of West Avenue.

Construction of the 5-storey office block,

Early Computers at ICL

When ICL started it was working with the legacy products from ICT and English Electric and had a total workforce in the UK of 34,000 - the largest computer firm outside the USA. The ICT machines were the *1900* series and from EE came the *System 4* and *M2000* ranges. It was clear that ICL needed to develop a new range and the 2900 series was launched in October 1974 after a long, six-year development programme where some £40 million was provided by the government. For the remainder of the 1970's ICL prospered and grew.

List of Computers

A list of some of the Mainframes made by ICL.

Model	Year
1908A	
2903	1973
2970	1974
2960	
2980	1975
2950	1978
DAP	1979
DRS 20	1981
MiniDAP	1985
39 Series	1990's

PCs
In addition to mainframes ICL also made PCs from 1982 such as the 15,25,26 and 35 models all based around the Intel 8085 microprocessor.

PCB Manufacture

As well as making computers the Kidsgrove factory made the Printed Circuit Boards - including the actual blank PCBs. A massive PCB plant carried out all the functions from etching of copper, cleaning, plating, drilling and so on to complete the finished boards.

The illustration above (taken in 1990) shows part of the PCB line which had 20 stages and used some 109 different chemicals! The blank boards were then populated using the most modern, automatic insertion/placement machinery available and soldered down. A few years after this picture was taken the PCB plant was decommissioned (when the firm was called D2D) and PCBs were then bought in.

Assembly of the main Series 39 Mainframe PCBs

Acquisitions, Take-overs and Mergers

The pace of computer development has always been fast and by the end of the 1970's ICLs machines were losing ground to the competition. A new range was required which would need many millions in development money. At the same time the country was going through a recession and profits were falling. The new conservative government under Thatcher was not going to provide free help as had the Wilson regime in the 1960's and money was raised from shareholders and bankers. Major restructuring took place from 1981 - 84 and the group went from 33,000 workers to 20,000. ICL decided they needed to have a partner who could bring new technology to their designs and negotiations were started with the Japanese firm Fujitsu who would provide the chips needed for the new 3900 series mainframe. At the same time ICL started talking to STC as it needed a partner in the telecommunications sector to prepare for the coming merger of IT and communication technology and the Internet.

These negotiations were to backfire on ICL which would eventually be swallowed up by both these partners. In 1984 STC acquired ICL by take-over and the UK s biggest player in computers became just another division of STC. STC soon reorganised ICL and set up Kidsgrove works as a manufacturing unit called D2D (Design to Distribution). The main ICL sign on the works was removed and replaced with D2D (although ICL still had a smaller presence on the site).

D2D would now concentrate on electronics sub-contract manufacture which started to change the whole direction of the firm. In 1990 the chip partner Fujitsu returned and bought up 80% ownership of ICL.

In 1991 the parent firm acquired part of Nokia and soon the Kidsgrove works would be building mobile phones, satellites, lottery terminals and a wide range of other products.

This situation continued up to January of 1997 when D2D was sold to the Canadian firm Celestica - a giant, sub-contract electronics manufacturer. By now - the old firm of ICL no longer owned any manufacturing plant directly (although ICL did maintain a small presence as part of the Celestica site).

Celestica at Kidsgrove continued to prosper and expand throughout the remainder of the decade until another recession - this time in the mobile communication market would hit in 2001.

Hundreds of redundancies were announced in the second half of 2001 as orders continued to fall. Even with a reduced workforce the site still remained a major employer in the area at the cutting edge of technology.

> In January 2002, it was announced in the press that the small, remaining ICL presence at Kidsgrove would be re-locating to the Crewe Business Park by 2003.
>
> It was also announced that the name ICL would be dropped as a brand name completely by Fujitsu thus marking the end of the ICL era.

Demolition of the old ICL Works - Summer 2005

Glossary of Terms and Abbreviations

2Q	Two Quadrant - Forward and Reverse Motoring, braking energy can not be returned to the supply and is lost as heat via braking resistors
4Q	Four Quadrant - Forward and Reverse Motoring plus Forward and Reverse Braking/Regeneration
AC	Alternating Current
AEM	Active Energy Management (MV3000 name for AFE - see below)
AFE	Active Front End - in a 4 quadrant converter power can be returned to the mains supply via the input bridge which has transistors or IGBTs instead of diodes
AVR	Automatic Voltage Regulator - complex cubicle based system for controlling the output of a large generator and one of the key products at Kidsgrove in the early years
CDC	Common Drive Controller - replaced the OMEGA and SIGMA controllers when the MV3000 range was introduced
DC	Direct Current
DELTA	The name given to the power bridge concept comprising of 3 SKiiP modules, capacitor bank and interface circuit
DIB	Delta Interface Board
DP	Data Processing (Division of EE)
EE	English Electric
EEC	English Electric Company
EEPROM	Electrically Erasable Programmable Read Only Memory
GEC	The General Electric Company Ltd, founded in England in 1889
ICL	International Computers Ltd
IGBT	Insulated Gate Bipolar Transistor
LCD	Liquid Cooled Delta
PCB	Printed Circuit Board
PLC	Programmable Logic Controller
PWM	Pulse Width Modulation
SCR	Silicon Controlled Rectifier = Thyristor
SKiiP®	Semikron Intelligent Power Module
Switching Frequency	The number of cycles per second of the PWM waveform. Not to be confused with the output frequency of the simulated sinewave produced by the PWM.
VVVF	Variable Voltage Variable Frequency - a method of motor control using a drive